The Rising Son

The story of a boy, a pub, a war and a remarkable woman

by
James Kelso

authorHOUSE™

1663 LIBERTY DRIVE, SUITE 200
BLOOMINGTON, INDIANA 47403
(800) 839-8640
WWW.AUTHORHOUSE.COM

First published by AuthorHouse 01/17/06

ISBN: 1-4208-9437-4 (sc)
ISBN: 1-4208-9438-2 (dj)

Printed in the United States of America
Bloomington, Indiana

This book is printed on acid-free paper.

To

'…the lot of youse…'

Contents

Chapter I
Here comes the son.

For the life of me, I can't remember my earliest recollection, though I've tried really hard. I admit this may not be the most promising way to begin a memoir, but the truth is those early years are a closed book to me - another unfortunate metaphor to put in your mind at the outset. So let me tell you what I was told. I was born in a small, private nursing home, near the Doll's Hospital, a toy shop in Fulham Road, London. It may have been in Dawes Road - the shop, not the birth - but the plot doesn't hinge on it and, like much that follows, it's not vital. Even the year doesn't matter, as I didn't know it at the time. Our dates may be brief, they're also misleading. You see them on gravestones: 'so-and-so, 1896-1983' and you might idly think to yourself, 1896, what happened back then? Was that the year of such-and-such? You then link the departed with whatever you've recalled as if they were part of it. But they knew nothing about it until years later. They were no more there in 1896 than you were. We come into the world in a fog and often leave in one. Maybe one day, with a few genetic tweaks, babies will be born sentient and formatted, knowing they're in Fulham and already wishing they weren't.

4654? Maybe that's the first memory, Fulham 4654. That was our phone number. We weren't digitised then. Baptised, yes, digitised, no. For though the rising son was born away from home, he was soon taken to his spiritual birthplace, The Rising Sun, a Watney house. This stood on the corner of Fulham Road and Holmead Road, opposite the main gates of Chelsea Football Club.

Watney, Coombe and Reid to be precise. This trio, along with much else of that time, have 'all gone into the dark'. Reid, I recall, had a stout named after him - or her. Reid's Stout, a dark, bottled beer that arrived in stout wooden crates, two dozen up.

The infant, you see, was born to licensed victuallers.

The telephone was on the landing, a room-sized area that was the main crossing point of home. Rooms and passages radiated from it like people walking away from an argument. My father was speaking on the phone. My mother and other people were gathered around, deedily talking, their conversation muted and ominous. The gravity of the moment conveyed itself even to the child lying on its back on the floor.

How big it all seemed. The towering figures. The tent-shaped glass fanlight that ran the length of the ceiling. It would be an atrium now. It was no atrium then. Indeed, it was on its way to becoming a blackout hazard.

Behind the child's head was the tallboy upon which, every spring, would stand a blue hyacinth proclaiming the season with its perfume. Of the tallboy's drawers, some were openable. Others were stuck so fast Samson himself could not have wrenched them free. Occasionally, if you gave a massive pull on the double wooden knobs, a drawer would break loose, rattling the hyacinth in its saucer and catapulting the contents out in a barrage of flying cotton reels and other haberdashery.

To the left was the hall table with its burden of cut-glass bowls, vases and silverware; lots of silverware, plates, cups and trophies, all speaking of a sporting heritage. The scent of Bluebell silver polish hung in the air, its nosegay going at it one-all with the hyacinth. On the table's lower level, between the fretworks at each end, lived the portable, red leather covered wind-up gramophone. Beside this was a pile of easy-to-break records. If the prone child - he'd turned on to his front by now - had stretched out its right arm, its hand would have touched the cold steel of the safe. This was a proper safe, impregnable; a cabinet of immense weight, table high and of a volume equal to the lower half of a telephone kiosk. It was painted dark, keep out green. On its imposing front were two handles, a key plate and a maker's nameplate, all shining brass. One handle was L-shaped. This operated the door's dual steel tongues, which engaged into deep apertures within the safe's inner walls. The other handle was round and fluted. With this you opened or closed the door, pulled or pushed, felt its weight, enjoyed its precision, heard the whisper of locked air as it sighed or gasped as it was imprisoned or released. The key plate was a shield-shaped flap which when lifted took the maleness of the key, covered its doings and applauded its exit with a light, clicking double bounce. This left only the nameplate, the plate remembered, the name forgotten. It bore a coat of arms, authoritative, impressive to an impressionable mind. The smell of Brasso lingered. Yellow dusters could not be far away.

Beyond the child's feet was the wall-mounted telephone. This had a separate earpiece; a black trumpet which, at rest, hung vertically from a Y-shaped hook. The mouthpiece was fixed in position but was adjustable. You could align its mouth with yours. On top of the instrument were twin electric bells that each had small exterior clappers. When the phone rang they went like the clappers they were. These were the bells to which we were summoned. This was how our phone declared itself.

On this occasion it was apparently declaring war.

Chapter II
My real father.

The first significant life claimed by the war that followed was that of my father. And, in so far as he lives in my memory, his was a short life.

I have only three recollections of him.

The first is that telephone call. The second is of a lunchtime, a Saturday I would guess, when we were downstairs in one of The Rising Sun's four bars, the main saloon. We were standing round the customer side of the counter. This, during opening hours, was forbidden and supremely exciting territory for the child to whom the whole of the public house was, at that age, out of bounds. My father was leaning with his back to the counter flap, near the square wooden pillar. He was smiling and proud, full of teetotal health, talking of his son, showing him off. The boy had been programmed to do a party trick. This was to give a recitation. The ritual was for the boy to stand to attention and recite a poem:

'There's a Cupboard Under the Stairs', by Willoughby.

The boy would then bow to his audience and begin. 'There's a cupboard under the stairs, with lions and tigers and bears ...' On this occasion the child had just been through this torture. The woodwork, the glassware, the very floor shone and gleamed with approval. All was cleanliness and wellbeing. The twin doors of the bar were open to the sunlit world outside, welcoming the thirsty of which, so far, only one had arrived.

He was Charlie Harris, a portly man of middle years who sported a porkpie hat, double chins, a waistcoat, a fob watch with a chain and kit-sized bags under his eyes. He lived above the greengrocer's a few doors along, a shop with a worn wooden planking floor, dusted heavily with earth from the hessian sacks full of cabbages and sprouts which fought for space with rickety wooden boxes of apples and other fruits and vegetables. The shop was from an earlier age, old-fashioned even then. Charlie Harris was a star in our firmament. He was, no less, the trainer, or was it assistant trainer, of Chelsea F.C.

The infant had been given some chewing gum.

'Don't chew that,' said Charlie Harris. 'You'll swallow it and it'll wrap itself around your heart and you'll die.'

The two grown-ups beamed down. The child felt the gum clutch his heart. Gum and heart were both now in his mouth. Benign smiles were smiled upon him. How the gum was supposed to have reached his heart was not explained. Perhaps it was Charlie Harris's knowledge of anatomy that accounted for Chelsea's position in the league at that time.

The third memory of my father is a confusion, I suspect, of one or more events joined as in a dream. My parent's bedroom was off the landing. The house itself was on the corner of the block and their room was the corner of the house. It was spacious, high ceilinged, airy and lit by two big windows. The window overlooking Fulham Road was huge, reaching from the ceiling almost to the floor. Lace curtains hung the full length, with other heavy drapes, rose pink, at each side. There was much furniture.

A fireplace with a mantelpiece and mirror above was in the centre of the Holmead Road wall. To the right, in the curve of the corner, sat a large armchair, dependably floral patterned. To its right was the dressing table. This was a two-seater with an upholstered bench seat. The wide mirror could be tilted and positioned, held between the slender wooden posts at each side by twin butterfly wing nuts. The table top was covered with glass, cut and shaped to the double kidney curves of the ensemble. Beneath the glass was more lace. Upon the glass top of the table was a much-prized dressing table set. There were tortoiseshell combs, mother-of-pearl backed brushes and a mother-of-pearl backed long-handled hand mirror. There was a jewellery casket, trinket boxes, powder puffs, a manicure set and cut glass perfume bottles with spray nozzles, the pressure supplied by squeezing a rubber bulb covered in tassels. Many fluid ounces of the perfume had, from time to time, been jetted by small hands at the family mongrel, effecting a marked improvement.

Dominating the room was a large double bed. A bed so high, a child had to climb up on to it, stepping on the iron metal of its substantial frame that itself stood two feet off the ground. Above this was a massive box mattress and on top of that another mattress. The bed boasted a polished wooden headboard with a tiny, silly, bed lamp mounted top centre, containing a bare bulb that had singed brown the parchment-like paper of its shade. There was an equally substantial footboard to the bed. It stood chest high to a man. This was some cot, a ship of the night on which to sail away.

My father, Philip Wade Kelso, lay in it, about to cast off.

It was night-time. The child was beside the bed, his father's hand near to him, his mother standing round the other side.

'Can't you hear the band?' my father said. 'Go to the window. See the band! They're marching by!'

The boy ran to the window. His sister, four years older, was sitting nearby. There was no band, no music. Again my father spoke.

'Fetch me the eagle. It's there on the curtains. Fetch it, fetch it.'

Like the band, like the music, there was no eagle, search though the boy did, small fingers rasping in the dry folds of the embroidered lace. Now the little boy sat on his sister's lap. They were both crying. The curtains were pulled back and they looked out into the lamp lit street. His sister comforted him, as she was to do many times in future. They watched an ambulance pull away, white with a blue light, its bell, which should have tolled, didn't. Ambulances had bells then, not hee-haw sirens. Their bells were tinny, hand-bellish, not deep toned, not significant. The children were now alone in the room. The big bed was empty, never to be filled in the same way again.

Alcoholic delirium tremens is puzzling to a six-year old.

My father remains the vague, shadowy figure he ever was, despite occasionally, and with increasing frequency, peering at me from my mirror where he vies with my mother in a ghastly take-over battle for my features. My distaste of this, my own regression, has nothing to do with my feelings towards these parental predators. They are merely doing what I shall no doubt do, reclaiming that which they made, retaking that which was once their own, insider trading with a vengeance. I can no more stand the thought of it than, so I surmise, my father could stand the thought of war.

Chapter III
Exit, followed by springbok.

Odd name, Wade.

To today's ear it has a touch of the tabloids about it. But for all I know, it may have a perfectly ordinary pedigree. It may be an old Scots forename, kilted and respectable, for my father was a Scot, a lowlander from Largs. Or perhaps it was an old surname, passed on for family reasons. I don't know. We're in research-free country here. Apocryphy without apology; our authenticity is our lack of authenticity.

The same with the death certificate. Heart failure was given as the cause, so I've been told, but I've never checked. As to why the heart failed? Whisky. And as to why the whisky? War. So I suspect. Remember, I was no more there than you were.

In later life, an osteopath once said to me: 'If everyone was built like you, there'd be no such thing as ballet.' If he'd looked at my tonsils he would have seen there would have been no opera, either. And if he'd examined my backbone - which he

10

happened to be doing at the time - he might have observed there's little of the warrior class about it. So to the whisky.

Philip Wade Kelso was too young to serve in the First World War and too old to serve in the Second. I have no idea if he considered this good or ill fortune. But the Second World War was, of course, the first world war in which the civilian population was the target of air raids. Myth has it that the citizens of the time were uniformly dipped in a Churchillian vat of stoicism in order to withstand the onslaught. Some, given the choice, may have dipped into a different vat, VAT 69, if they could get their hands on a few bottles. And if you lived in a pub, you could.

There was also a peer of the realm involved. More hearsay now, or her say I should say, for this was my mother's tale to me, to us, as I recall. Opposite the pub, in Fulham Road there lay behind studded, oaken double doors set in a high white wall, an Italianate village, a London Portmerion called Chelsea Studios. That's where the peer lived. He was, for all I know, too young for the first and too old for the second and so on. He bore a famous name, the son of a famous father, and he liked a snort after closing time.

The peer rarely spent the meat of the evening in SW6 and who could blame him? But late at night, if all was quiet on the West One front, he would return prepared to slum it with the locals, including Dad. And with the natural confidence of the aristocracy, secure in the danger of those strange, theatrical times and, no doubt, bolstered by a fluid ounce or two of the necessary, he was not above rapping on the windows, if the blacked-out lights were still on, or failing that, he'd ring the private door bell, the large round, electric bell push which was set high up in the yellow tiles to the left of the inset porch of number 477.

Whether he got the, good evening m'lud, I don't know. But he was made welcome, so it seems. He, so Mum said, taught Dad to drink. And Dad, getting a taste of what he'd been missing these forty-two years, went at it with a will. He filled the cup and not so slowly drowned himself to death. It only took a year. Sometimes, in the middle of the night, he could be found, sitting alone, slumped in the lower corner of the stairs, still drinking even after his lordship had gone home. 'Come to bed,' mother would call down to him. But he never came. Nothing could deflect him from his chosen path. Not even the love of his two children whom, I'm told, he adored. That my father did the deed, I do know. Why he did it, I don't know.

To guess that it was fear of the war is unfair on him. Probably most people were frightened at the time, not unreasonably so, with bombs being dropped on them every night. As to what other arrows were being slung his way around this period, I've no idea. But I do know one thing that must have upset him mightily. That was the matter of his own dad, Old Man Kelso, my grandfather. The fact is my father couldn't stand up to his father.

This wasn't surprising. Old Man Kelso, whose first name was also Philip, was by all accounts, a 'stern, abrasive Scot', a 'disciplinarian' with 'firm views'. He was prosperous, successful and powerful. He'd been a football club manager. First with Hibernian, then for four years with Arsenal - he was their manager when they moved from Woolwich to Highbury - finally he was with Fulham for fifteen years. He'd also owned or managed a hotel in Largs; then the Grove Tavern in Hammersmith Grove and, of course, The Rising Sun. He must have been fit. In an emergency during the First World War he played for Fulham aged 47! He also played golf to an international standard.

His was the sporting heritage in the family. His were the big silver cups, the small silver cups, the silver platters, the silver cigar cases ribbed to take five fat Havanas, the plush-lined leather bound boxes, soft with velvet, and nestled in them timeless and beribboned medals.

Philip Kelso, winner of this; Philip Kelso, winner of that; Philip Kelso first; Philip Kelso second; Philip Kelso third. His name was everywhere, engraved and embossed on polished surfaces; surfaces that curve and distort your own reflection as you look, especially as you look back.

One splendid cup I recall was a three-parter: on top was a fine round pot complete with removable lid. From the pot's base, three slim legs tapered downwards and inwards to a further separate base. On this stood a three-inch high silver golfer, head impeccably down, club impeccably up, frozen in a shining, plus-four'd back swing, a tiny silver ball at his feet. The whole thing was perched on an ebony plinth with a green baize base. The whole thing was also regularly sent flying by a certain member of the upcoming generation, who earned himself many reproofs in the process.

Among all these distorting mirrors the runners up in these events, the family Kelso, went about their daily business. They loomed, grew immense, and passed by to become tiny again. There were also many framed photographs and newspaper sports cartoons of the great man hung in the two saloon bars of The Rising Sun. Other faded photographs show him behind the bar - not working, of course - with a group of people, including my father. Dad is holding the FA Charity Shield Trophy. What this occasion was, I know not. Yet another print shows the last drama, Old Man Kelso's funeral cortege heading along Fulham Broadway towards his 'cup final', the urn.

'They even switched off the traffic lights for him,' Mum would say with bitter pride.

All in all, it appears he was a swell, pot bellied, mustachioed and gold fob watch chain amidships.

'He took ten pounds out of the till every morning and that would be the last we'd see of him for the day,' Mum used to say.

Good riddance, she may have added, for she certainly did not like him, or the rest of his family. She did not like him because of what he had done to his son, her husband, and to her. And what he had done was this.

My father was trained and worked as an engineer. He met my mother just where the Fulham Road joins the Fulham Palace Road. This meeting was often recounted to me. They were walking in opposite directions on the same pavement. They passed each other by, both turned for a second look and begad I was begot. They married and lived happily for a while in a flat in one of those quiet, leafy streets near the Bishop of Fulham's Palace. That home was my mother's first proper home of her own and it was to remain her spiritual home, her palace, for the rest of her life.

But along came fob watch amidships. Things it seems were tough in the pub business. The Old Man wanted his son to come and live and work in the pub. Such was the filial tie, the sense of duty, this came to pass. The quiet leafy days were put behind the young couple. The home of their own was given up. The engineer became a barman. His wife, I believe, never forgave him. And within a few short years he was dead. One effect of his early exit from the plot was to bind his male heir in a cat's cradle of maternal apron strings, a knot that to this day the grown infant has not unknotted nor outgrown. So much for my father. I never had the chance to speak to him, man to man, so to speak. So I do so now. Hello, Dad. Good-bye, Dad.

Chapter IV
My unreal father.

Good-bye Dad, hello Reginald Osborne from South Africa. Uncle Reg, as he became known, with the constant refrain from Mum: 'He's not your real father you know'. Well, I didn't know and I didn't care. I loved him as much as if he was my real father. And, as far as I can tell, he loved me as much as if I was his real son. He was the male part of the team that brought me up. He not only brought me up, he slung me downstairs once. But that was much later, when I was well deserving of correction.

How he came into the land of The Rising Sun is, I believe, because he often came into The Rising Sun to drink. It was one of his haunts. He was, I like to think, footloose and fancy free. An entirely proper condition for a gentleman of the type known, in those far off days, as a bachelor. A fine title for a noble state. He lived in Worcester Park and worked as a salesman, selling sun blinds and shop front awnings, for Dean's Blinds of Putney.

Reg was regularly joined in his D'Artagnan revels by two other musketeers, Jan Janaway and Dodger Green. When this trio were on the spree, esprit was in the air. The earth shook. The Sun shook. Janaway certainly shook. He had a laugh - more of a bray - that could be heard in Bray. He also had a favourite and highly unlikely party trick. He could, astoundingly, recite whole tracts of the Bible. This was not a text regularly heard in the top saloon, one of the Sun's four bars. While Janaway gave chapter and verse to anyone who cared to listen - and you could hear him half way down the King's Road in distant World's End - Dodger, slick, dapper, moustached, bow-tied - wouldn't you know it - oiled his way around, floating on a cloud of after-shave. This was in the days before after-shave. It was almost before shaving. This eminent trio was augmented to quartet status on special occasions by one, Swanee, who hailed from parts even more distant than World's End, the far away reaches of Watford or thereabouts.

Though Janaway and Dodger were Reg's regulars, they were by no means his only team. Far from it. Reg had a past, he had history. He was born in South Africa, in East London was it? How he finished up in west London, I don't know. Reg only illuminated South Africa once, much later, when I was at school and one evening was doing some homework.

'What subject?' he asked.

'History,' I said, 'the story of Paul Kruger and the founding of the Orange Free State.'

'He used to live opposite me,' he said. Sometimes a history lesson just comes to life.

Reg and his brother Frank had both been professional footballers. Reg played left back for Leicester City. Frank was a left-winger. They'd both played for England, the last brothers to do so - I think - before Gary and Phil Neville in the modern era. While Reg was presently engaged in playing a blinder for Dean's, Frank, following in the footsteps of Old Man Kelso, was at this time - or maybe a bit later - manager of Fulham Football Club. Frank was not much on the scene. It was the terrible trio who were most in evidence. Somehow, through their regular performances in the top saloon, Reg it seems, became best friends with my father. What more natural then, with the threat of war looming, that at one point Dad is reputed to have asked Reg to promise to 'look after the family, if anything should happen to me.'

What best friend could refuse such a request? And barring the accidents of war, what could happen to a fit, teetotal 40-year-old, a man in his prime? If ever there was a marker that wasn't going to be called in, this was it. I can imagine Reg's reply.

'Sure, yes, of course, don't you worry, a pleasure, flattered to be asked' and so on.

So it was that later, one death later, the marker was called in. Quite how Mum 'snaked him in out of the wet' I'm not sure, but snake him in she did. From the sunshine and the awnings and the wide-open spaces of Worcester Park, in he came to the dark world of cellars, of tapping kegs, of bunging bungs in firkins and rolling out the barrels. A life sentence behind bars.

Of course, in due course, they married. There was a delay in making the actual arrangements, a slight interregnum. A quarter of a century to be precise but one doesn't want to rush these things. It would be kindly to flesh out the details of the coming together, the romance, if there was one. The attraction, the lone grieving widow, the handsome, honourable friend, offering each other shelter amid the dark clouds of conflict. The simple truth is I don't know the mills and boon of it. I do know Reg was suddenly among us, as natural as air. His was the spare bedroom, off the hall, opposite the safe. A safe room in a safe house. I never saw him in any other bedroom. I never witnessed even the briefest of encounters.

In those pre-Philip Larkin days, sex hadn't yet been invented. Licensing laws had though. And, though a marriage licence was decades down the line, a licence to run the Sun was a matter of urgency. Back then, a woman was not allowed to hold a licence to sell wines and spirits. Women weren't thought worthy to be licensed victuallers. With Dad gone, Mum was faced with eviction. But there was a war on. Exceptional circumstances.

Normally a big, profitable pub in a prime location outside a football ground would have applicants queuing to run it. But at the time most of the eligible men were engaged on other duties, in Dunkirk and so on. Could the bereaved widow of the licensee, in these special times, be considered worthy of taking over and holding a license? Certainly not. Well, certainly not without a man in the house.

Mmm! How to get round that one? Up some ladder somewhere, a happy awning salesman didn't realise a new world was dawning for him. And so it was that Mrs Cecilia Ann Kelso, née Millard, became one of, if not the first, of Watney's female licensees.

I wonder how romantic that moment was when Mum asked Reg to come and live in? It was obviously a dramatic and significant decision for both of them. I wonder what he said? Probably:

'Kraigs-ghy-fagin-agin-laager.'

Reg, you see, was a man of habits. And one of his habits was to say strange words over and over again. Kraigs-ghy-fagin-agin-laager was one of these. Don't ask me what it means or how to spell it. I've never seen it written down. I've guessed at this spelling, just to give it a touch of the veldt. I can tell you how Reg pronounced it:

Kraigs, as in Craig's; ghy, as in dinghy; fagin, as in Dickens; agin, as in fagin; and laager as in lager.

Kraigs-ghy-fagin-agin-laager. What could be simpler? I have long kept an ear out for an explanation of this oddity, but with no luck. Perhaps it's the name of a river, some natural feature, some commonplace thing. The world's search engines are silent on the subject. Reg, however, wasn't. He said it often. Very, very often. And after hearing the word repeated 20 million times, I emigrated to Norway, to pose for Edvard Munch's painting known as 'The Scream' and, while modelling, endlessly repeated my other childhood mantra:

'He's not your real father, you know.'

Barrels were not the only thing Reg tapped. Another of his pastimes, another of his grate habits, was to tap the dog's basket with the tip of his shoe. Tap, tap, tap. You know the old saying, let sleeping dog's lie? Well, Reg didn't. He tapped, tapped, tapped until the dog snapped and bit at the offending shoe. Reg's sportsman's reflexes meant the toecap was always withdrawn in time. In turn, this meant the dog missed the shoe and invariably bit the edge of its basket. Bits would be bitten out. The basket would gradually be reduced to its woven floor, with its doggy blanket, and a ring of surrounding gnawed uprights. We went through many baskets and a number of neurotic dogs. How many is not important because they've all morphed into one. They were all mongrels, small wire-haired terrier-type things. I loved them with equal passion. They all looked the same and they were all called Dur-Dur.

Yes, yes, I know, you couldn't make it up.

Reg's ways with words and dogs were not the only trials that dogged his new family. Reg disagreed. He disagreed with everything. He was a professional disagreer. He did so in a benign way. I don't recall giant rows on specific subjects. It was more attitudinal, a general approach to the world and its ways and conversation in particular. You know those broadcasts where interviewers roast politicians? If the victim is on the left, the questions come from the right. If the victim is on the right, the questions come from the left. It's adroit, even if it does leave you wondering what the elected representatives might have said if left to their own devices. Well Reg, of course, wasn't in that league. He operated on a more humdrum level. He just disagreed in a mildly cantankerous, amiable sort of way, with everybody. His was idle, purposeless contradiction. Which was fair enough. You always knew where you stood. You always knew where he stood. This made for a certain solidity; it was a comfort, a rock upon which one could stand. It also accounted for why Uncle Reg was known by Mum and others in the family unit, including the dog, as Tommy Oppo.

Chapter V
And other animals.

With Tommy Oppo on board, the threat of being driven to nervous distraction increased, but the threat of eviction from The Sun receded. This must have been a relief to all concerned. The young master, however, took it in his stride not knowing the threat existed. He carried on as before, getting around at trip-over-him height, supremely contented. One reason for his contentment, apart from his ever-present loving Mum, was his equally ever-present loving sister, Margaret, four years his senior.

Marg, as she was known then - with a hard g as in dinghy - is an elusive figure in my memory of that time. The bond between us has always been indissoluble. It seems disrespectful to say it, but the truth is I don't remember much of our days together back then. It's more like Margaret was always there, always on my side. She never slung me down stairs or anything like that. We're like those entangled particles physicists talk about, that know what the other is doing even though they're on opposite sides of the universe. We're not that far apart, Margaret lives in Hounslow. Towards adolescence the rows and arguments we had, so I've been told, were stupendous. Uncle Reg once said they named the Great Rift Valley in East Africa after us. For my part, I don't remember. To this day we share gales of laughter mainly caused by our amazement at what went on in those early years.

So there we were, Mum, Reg, Marg, me, the dog and of course the Mickeys.

The Mickeys were cats, à la Dur-Dur, the name remained, the embodiment came and went. The Mickeys only ever sat in two places. One was on the shelf behind the taps of the kitchen sink, where it, or they, could moult into the washing up. The other favourite place was on the windowsill in the little room. The little room was the small sitting room at the end of the small passage past the door to, you guessed it, the big room. When the little room window was thrown up, the sun streamed in, the Mickeys basked, and Mum counted the money. Doing the tills, it was called. Cashing up, you might say. Everything was cash in those half-a-crown years. Once a week all four tills, the top saloon, two main saloons, one public bar, had to be reconciled. Mum would turn over the heavy embroidered tablecloth so as not to dirty the top, lay the coin on the underside, and quietly count away. And a grand spread it was: the tanners, the shillings, the florins, the three-penny bits, the ten-bob notes, the great white fivers. The currency was arranged into families, then bagged up into stout paper bags, different colours for different denominations, ready for the next delivery to the bank; Barclays Bank, Munster Road. Sometimes I'd get to ride shotgun on those paying-in visits but I didn't relish it. The cloth moneybags weighed a ton. Is the bank still there? I don't know. It has probably been stolen.

The little room window opened on to the roof garden. The roof garden! You estate agent! It was about as much of a roof garden as nearby Eel Brook Common was like Versailles. The roof garden was slab of easy-melt asphalt about the size of half a tennis court. Two-thirds of the area was taken up by a chest high, glass box-like affair, with vertical windows and a sloping roof. This was a roof light. It was the lungs of the main saloon bar. When its vertical windows were pivoted open, an immense plume of tobacco smoke rose upon the evening air, taking with it a good portion of the lungs of the revellers below.

The remainder of the roof was covered, wall-to-edge, with wooden slats mounted on cross bars. This was an early form of decking, a very, very early form. The slats were there to prevent strollers from sinking without trace in the asphalt quagmire. The gaps in the slats were just wide enough to accept a dog's doings provided it was deposited in the correct orientation. Nature, of course, is resourceful. Dur-Durs, one and all, were programmed to hit the spot unerringly. Uncanny. And, of course, if mere dogs can do it, well, what self-respecting cat would want to be left out of the grand design. The Mickeys joined in with a will.

The local atmosphere was further enriched by the proximity of an open-roofed urinal. It was one of ours, it just happened to be outside. The saloon bar toilets were highly civilised and indoor but public bar patrons enjoyed the great outdoors. From the roof, if you craned your neck, you could look down on them at their labours. And their labours, in tandem with the slats, lent to the air of the garden a certain, shall we say, personality. On hot summer days even the plume of smoke wouldn't come out to play. Once in a while, when sufficient residents of the surrounding postal district had passed out with the smell, a giant roof clean was initiated. This was a daylong task and meant lifting the massive 12-foot long grids of slats and evacuating the evacuations.

While this work was in progress, the cat would bask on the windowsill, the dog would keep one eye on proceedings, both quietly digesting, both knowing the labour was in vain. This may have been where Reg got the idea for toe-tapping the basket.

The garden may not have been fragrant, but it did have a ha-ha! This was more of a four-foot drop, a step down on to a lower roof on the north side. This part of the roof overlooked

Frenchy's Yard. It too had a roof light. You probably don't want to know this light was above the civilised indoor facilities for saloon bar customers. You probably also don't want to learn that below this roof, at ground level, was where the establishment's dustbins were kept. Surely we've had enough obnoxious effluvia. Enough what? Obnoxious effluvia! That was one of Mum's sayings. 'What an obnoxious effluvia,' she'd say, when the dog walked passed dragging its odour plume with it. Where did she get that phrase? Out of a book? I don't remember seeing many books about the place. I recall many obnoxious effluviums - if that's the plural - but not books. There was one noble exception:

Jeeves Omnibus, by P.G.Wodehouse, '... no comparison as a missile in an inter-study brawl.'

A low brick wall, topped with a chain link fence, bordered the west side of the roof. The drop beyond was huge and the view spectacular. You know Lucian Freud's painting, 'Waste ground with houses, Paddington'? It was like that but more interesting. You looked out over the back gardens of our neighbours. First, the Misses Jackson - I think there were three - owners of the sweet shop next door. Then Mr Davis, newsagent with his gammy leg, purveyor of the Daily Mirror and Daily Express, our journals of record. Beyond him, the Blanks, of whom I have no recall. Then came the milk shop. Then the greengrocer, above which Charlie Harris lodged. Finally, on the other corner of the block by the bridge, The Stamford Arms, another pub. The gardens were graced with many fine trees, plane trees I guess, but mature and majestic, doing a fine job of shading Fulham from those endless summer suns. And away to the right, filling half the horizon with its pulsating grandeur, Lots Road Power Station. No wonder I was happy back then.

Beyond the trees, scarcely glimpsed behind summer's foliage but revealed in winter, the branch line of the railway, the steam railway, the fully operational, day and night working steam railway. Why the attraction to railways and other behind-the-fences worlds? Was it because they were our childhood playgrounds? The empty stations, the bombed sites, the derelict waste lands, disused overgrown sidings, goods yards and engine sheds, canal banks, vacant warehouses, the abandoned places where 'the ragged people go'? Brown-field sites they call them now. They weren't brown. They glowed with rose bay willow herb, flowering amid the dust, flourishing in the cinders and the potash, waving and dancing in the polluted air.

Was it the music, the sibilance of steam, the rhythm of the rails, ter-tum, ter-tum, der-dun, der-dun? The shriek of wheel flange on tortured steel, the iron clink-clank pat-a-cake of wagon on coupled wagon?

Or maybe I was star struck. These locations were film stars. They were in almost every British movie, woven into smoky, brooding tapestries, a black and white romance language born of the need for filmmakers to escape public places and work uninterrupted. These empty plots spoke with silent eloquence of their times, while the stage of daily life, the roads and streets, the greengrocers and newsagents, the milk shops and pavements, slipped anonymously away, out of sight, almost unrecorded.

And a good job too! That was another of Mum's sayings, 'a good job too!'

However, despite the attractions of the roof and the siren song of shunting engines, life was not all lived outdoors. The Sun had another playground, the cellar.

Chapter VI
Descend lower.

In the first and second world wars, soldiers in battle wore tin hats. Our family, during air raids, wore tin baths. Are tin baths still made? I haven't seen one in years. I'd certainly recognize one, as on many occasions I wore one upturned on my head. I was not alone. There were usually one or two other heads sheltering inside with me. Tin baths were our last line of defence against the Junkers 88. In the early days of the war, when the blitz started, the air raids came at night. The cellar, with its ceiling of rolled steel joists - or were they just stout wood - became our refuge. There were beds down there, jammed in among the usual furniture of cellarage. There seemed to be many people. Who would have been there, apart from the immediate family and a few Dur-Durs? I imagine the-not-so-immediate family, who headed our way when the sirens went. Having a good cellar meant quite a different thing back then. I suppose there may even have been, from time to time, customers sharing the shelter. Certainly never Janaway and Dodger Green, I'd remember them all right. What do I recall of the danger and the fear? Nothing, I was too young. The drama passed me by. I can recall one or two ear-splitting bangs, and some earthshaking thumps, when dribbles of dust would fall from the ceiling on to the wooden crates of light ale. These explosions reverberated around the insides of the tin bath in an interesting harmonic way that stopped just short of melting your eyeballs.

Let's try a roll call.

Uncle Jack and Auntie Win with their brood, yes. Aunt Ethel and cousins Joan and Gerald, maybe. I say maybe because the story, put about by Uncle Reg so not necessarily to be trusted, was this. When the Prime Minister, Neville Chamberlain, made his famous broadcast announcing we were at war, Aunt Ethel, Joan and Gerald were having breakfast in their flat at 51 Moore Park Road. On hearing the news they put their knives and forks down, picked up their hats and coats and went to live with Uncle Ed and Aunt Thelma in Arundel, Sussex. Five years later they returned to No 51, washed up the plates and carried on as before. They said the egg yolk was hard to wash off. This adhesive power, I learned later, is the secret of tempera painting.

Were there any other refugees? There must have been but I can't name them.

Perhaps some of the pub staff? Dora maybe. Dora was the cook. This kind lady inadvertently furnished the young master with an indelible image he has long wished was delible. One day, when the three or four-year old infant was lying on his back on the kitchen floor, Dora chanced to step over him, her skirts spread wide, while she stretched up to some shelf or other. The child incuriously looked upwards. What he saw was remarkable. It was a scene, I assure you, of the utmost decorum. The garment displayed - and like the tin baths, I'm not sure if they are made any more - was a pair of what were called bloomers. These were a knicker-like arrangement that began at the knee and expanded upwards and outwards like airships, a pair of vertical low-flying Zeppelins. The satin material was fluted and folded, arching upwards and rouched here and there, no doubt because it had been sat in. The ensemble had a certain architectural elegance. Here was a great cathedral of bloomer, pink and shiny, vaulting to its conclusion like the ceiling of Kings College Chapel. The child had never seen anything like it. Mercifully he has never seen anything like it since.

Was big Pat Brady there in the cellar with us? I doubt it. I think he came on the scene later. When big Pat arrived, you noticed it. Pat Brady worked as a drayman for Watney. A lifetime devoted to single-handedly humping 36-gallon barrels had influenced his physique. He was planetary, a great bear of a man, a shire horse on tree trunk legs. His chest was double-barrelled. His fists were like hams, big hams, full hams. He had twinkling eyes and a smile as wide as the Bay of Tralee. If he was smiling. Which he usually was. But sometimes he wasn't. In Hammersmith, so it was said, his prodigious feats in the dance halls and bar rooms of the day had earned him a nickname among the indigenous community. He was known behind his back - a capacious zone - as the Wolf. He had a husky, slightly hoarse voice, low pitched. He spoke slowly, as if the sound took some time to traverse the cavern of his chest. His voice carried vast distances like whale song. One evening after closing time, he told the story of his family, his thirteen brothers and sisters who had spread world wide, an Irish diaspora. It was a luckless tale. Many, if not most, of the siblings had suffered all manner of appalling fates.

'The shaft of the pony cart, right through his chest,' Big Pat said, 'would you believe it, right the way through, in at the front, out at the back!'

One by one they fell, or were accounted for, until the final sister.

'Lost touch with her these thirty years, never so much as a letter, a phone call, not so much as a word, and that's the truth, so it is,' he lamented.

Where did she live someone asked?

'Earls Court,' said Big Pat.

Pat Brady worked for the Sun, part time, for many a long year. And though he lived in England down most of his days, he never left Ireland far behind. One famous week he didn't show up for work, nor call, nor give any warning, driving Uncle Reg wild. Then suddenly, there he was, as usual.

'Where have you been?' demanded Reg.

'I've been on nights for few days,' Big Pat explained.

Much later, if Mum and Reg went away for a week's holiday, Big Pat would stopover at the Sun and look after the place. When he did so, he took it upon himself to get the young master up in the mornings. He'd knock on my bedroom door, step in, bearing a mug of tea and the morning paper, and in his resonant basso profondo that distinguished him from the other whales, he'd boom:

'Drink your tea, read your paper, and get oop!'

If by then you were a rebellious teenager, full of yourself, anti-everything, hating authority, pushing against the envelope of the world, what did you do?

You drank your tea, you read your paper, and you got oop!

So, how often were we in the cellar? Every night? No, not often. I think I remember it because it was unusual rather than normal. Unusual is not perhaps the right word to use about an occasion when three or four people, of mixed ages, sat in bed with their heads in a tin bath. I don't mean to trivialize the danger, far from it. In fact, the risk was obviously increasing, because at some point a decision was taken to evacuate Margaret and I.

You will have seen newsreel footage of evacuees, the confused children in their caps and berets, coats and short trousers, labelled with their names, gas masks round their necks, pictured with distracted parents in the milling scrum of railway stations. Similar scenes, of course, were being acted out all over Europe with many grim and final destinations. My hatred for the regime that did this - and their neo-cousins of today - remains as much a danger to my present health as bombs were back then.

Happily, but not unshadowed, our version of evacuation was a more privatised affair. We went by coach, Green Line I believe, and headed northwest out of the city. I think we may have gone several times, returning at weekends or intervals. One journey I do recall. We passed along Park Lane by Marble Arch. An anti-aircraft battery with artillery guns and searchlights was based in Hyde Park. They were in action. The noise of the guns was stupefying, the lights and blinding flashes bone-shuddering. Can we really have been this close to the action? Memory says yes, common sense has its doubts.

Off we went then, heigh-ho, to our place of succour, the small hamlet where we came closer to being blown to bits by enemy action than at any other time during the war, Kinsbourne Green, Harpenden, Hertfordshire.

Chapter VII
Herts ease.

Actually, I think Wealdstone come before Harpenden, chronologically I mean. I think we were shipped out to the perceived safety of Wealdstone as an interim measure. We certainly went there for a while and it was certainly the place where I first met the Nazgul.

The Nazgul are the horrors in J.R.R.Tolkein's, Lord of the Rings. He hadn't invented them yet, but they were already manifest and, it seemed to me, multiplying. They were jack-booted, cloaked in black, and flew everywhere, trailing chains of ebony beads weighted with heavy iron crosses. They were nuns. This was war and I feared the monstrous anger of the nuns. They were cowled and scowled down on me as I cowered. The fact was, in the family's desire to shield their offspring, they had got me to a nunnery and I didn't like it. I had yet to learn the wartime truth pronounced by Nancy Mitford. Quoting her Uncle Matthew, she wrote:

'All nuns are spies - German parachutists - you can tell by their boots.'

That knowledge hadn't reached me yet. I was the only boy in this place of low-flying hooded figures. The fact meant nothing at that age. All I can remember is darkness and stained glass, overgrown ivy and rain-soaked flagstone paths, strange walkways canopied with glass. And the pictures, of course.

The walls were covered with bas-relief images of mutilated bodies oozing blood, butchered and disembodied hearts with severed arteries, jetting gouts of gore. There were many depictions of one poor chap, almost nude, he wore a loincloth and a grimace. He was also sporting a strange hat, worn at a rakish angle, with no crown and a brim made of thorns. He was nailed hand and foot to a wooden cross.

So, nothing odd about this place then.

I don't think we stayed long with the Nazguls. The years have been kind in that I recall little of the experience. It must have been some sort of boarding school, or house of correction. Perhaps it was the original sin bin. I must have been a diligent pupil in that they didn't nail me to anything. I got a few whacks from the flying iron crosses but so did many others.

The next stop in our search for safety was among the rolling hills of Hertfordshire in Kinsbourne's green and pleasant land. And a certain cesspit comes to mind, waiting, I fear, for its share of the limelight.

To reach the cottage that was to become our home was easy. From the bus stop on the main road, climb over the stile, across the big field peopled with cows and sometimes horses, avoid the open cesspit - of which more later, more's the pity - over the second stile and there they were: two semi-detached cottages, two-up, two-down, the staff quarters of the adjacent Royal Army Ordnance Corps depot. In the one on the left, lived Uncle Ralph, Sgt Ralph Porter, R.A.O.C., with his wife Auntie Kit and an incomputable host of children, siblings, cousins and a generous helping of sheltering aunts and sundry other drop-ins who'd stopped by for the duration. To this welcoming roster we were added.

I loved Uncle Ralph and Auntie Kit. They were brilliant to me, to all of us, and we were legion. Ralph and Kit had five children of their own. Celia, Patricia, Kitty, Winnie and Peggy, the last two names adding a certain Canadian lilt to morning register I always thought. I can also see Aunt Ethel and cousin Joan. Maybe they were on leave from Arundel or hadn't reached Sussex yet. Was Auntie Win there with any of her brood? Not sure. Now add Margaret and me and the cottage was on the point of putting up the no-room-at-the-inn sign.

The building really was tiny. Its footprint wasn't much bigger than mine. It had a postage stamp living room with a narrow flight of wooden stairs going up to the boudoirs. There was a front room, but I don't think it was used much. Maybe it was kept for best? I only recall being in there once, when I was ill in bed with a high temperature and fever. The doctor was called. I was suffering from wanting-to-be-with-my-Mum-itis, an ague that still afflicts me from time to time.

The kitchen had a coal-fired oven arrangement for cooking and heating. Bodies heated the rest of the house. Off the kitchen was a half-inside, half-outside room. It had a brick floor, stable doors and contained a copper, a large, waist-high circular affair used for boiling or washing. I remember an accident once with boiling water spilling over someone's bare leg. The leg swelled up like Dora's bloomers and the howls echoed down the valley. Maybe the room had once been a cattle byre. As well as the copper, the room was home to, you'll be pleased to know, a tin bath. And I was pleased to know I didn't have to wear it on my head although, as we'll see, it would have come in handy later. This bath was used for the Friday night bathing ritual. This was more akin to sheep dipping than the porcelain routines of today. While mulling over these ablution zones I realise I have no recollection of where the toilet was. That doesn't augur well does it? Perhaps that's why my synapses have put the block on it.

So, small house, large complement. Do you ever travel on the Northern Line, in the rush hour? That's how we lived. And with the exception of Uncle Ralph, who was on duty in the depot most of the time, I was the only boy in the place. Again, of no consequence, still too young dammit.

I can recall the sleeping arrangements with clarity. So would you if you'd been there. There were two bedrooms upstairs and these were packed like shipping containers. One was loaded with adults. The other contained children, several of whom were well into their teens. I was the smallest child and slept at the far end of what was, at night time, a sea of sleepers. If I sat up in bed, I could gaze across the endless rows of humped forms disappearing into the far darkness. I was also gazing across what was no doubt a hormonal maelstrom. It's just as well I was the only boy in the place or we may have procreated ourselves into starvation by the sheer force of propinquity.

How did Auntie Kit feed us all? These were the days of stringent rationing and she performed miracles. I can't imagine how she coped. She was a lovely woman, properly shaped like an aunt, with red rosy cheeks and a huge smile. For all I know we may have grazed on tree bark and other country delicacies. I'd like to say I don't remember ever being hungry, but I do. And it was while in this, our country retreat, I had three escapes from death.

One from greed. One from a dive. And one from a dive-bomber.

Chapter VIII
Herts not at ease.

The dive-bomber came one Sunday lunchtime. Sunday lunch was big news in the house; it was the roast meal of the week and much looked forward to. I seem to recall we ate in shifts. This Sunday, the first sitting was taking place in the tiny front room. Uncle Ralph was at his usual seat, head of the table, back to the front window. The air raid warning siren had sounded but this didn't bother us. We were used to it. Indeed, when far away London was being bombed we would often imagine we could see the glow of the fires in the night sky. Today was different. An aircraft was heard approaching, the noise growing louder.

Uncle Ralph stood up and looked out of the window.

'Down,' he shouted. 'Take cover!'

I was dragged under the table by many hands. There were already many people there on all fours, including Margaret and Aunt Ethel. High-speed rosaries were being recited. Several people were loudly hailing Mary. I didn't know the lady but it was clear she was in much demand. I was petrified. It wasn't the first time I'd been frightened. But it was the first time I found myself shuddering uncontrollably. The roar of the aircraft grew deafening. There was a tremendous explosion that blew in the kitchen window at the back.

Somebody yelled:

'Whitesox! Is Whitesox okay?'

I crawled out. Uncle Ralph was still standing by the window. I was still shuddering with fright. There was a tiny broom cupboard under the stairs. Its door creaked slowly open and, like the prisoners in Fidelio, a large number of people were released into the care of the community. They were all compressed. Some of the shorter ones were squeezed almost flat like ironing boards. It took most of the day before they'd expanded back to normal.

The bomb had landed some 250 yards away in the big field, the one with the cesspit. Whitesox was the name of the horse liveried there. The animal was unhurt and to prove it was galloping around the perimeter hedge at 100 mph. By nightfall it had slowed to a 30 mph cruise. The plane presumably had been targeting the military depot. It had dropped a stick of three bombs. They fell a huge distance apart, over half a mile between them we were told. Finding we were unhurt, the scramble began to rush out to see the crater and get some shrapnel souvenirs before they cooled. That's what you do. That's probably what children in Iraq are doing today.

My second dice with doom had a different flavour. Enter the cesspit. Regrettably I was about to. It was like this. It was the habit of the household to regularly send out raiding parties to buy shopping or do other chores, sometimes even to go to the cinema. I was normally lugged along on these outings. The shops, the cinema, all human life, were a bus ride away, so the outings involved the familiar route. Climb over the stile, cross the field, past the cesspit, dodge the cowpats, over the second stile and so on, a well-known path holding no surprises. On this occasion our braves were returning from a long maraud. It was late afternoon, growing dusk. The sun had gone, the mists were gathering, the 'lowing herd wound slowly o'er the lea'. Actually, the lowing herd was almost out of sight at the far end of the field. How many were there in the herd, 25, 30? What exactly is a herd? A large group of mammals living and feeding together. I believe we were eight in our party that night. This, I suppose, could be construed as a large group of mammals living and feeding together. You could certainly think of it that way if you were a cow at the far end of a field on a misty evening and thought you saw another herd on your patch.

Pure speculation of course. For some bovine reason, known only to them, the placid animals decided to stampede and charge the intruders. We, for our part, on hearing the drumming of hooves and feeling the shaking of the ground, entered into the spirit of the event. We too stampeded. You've heard of the bull running at Pamplona? It is nothing compared to this. If I were on the local district council I'd make this an annual event. I'd sell the global TV rights and pocket large sums for the needy. I'm not quite sure why, but the quarry in question, namely us, chose to leg it in line abreast, holding hands. This Riverdance routine, though no doubt elegant, slowed us considerably. We rapidly lost ground to the Friesians.

Of course, you know what's coming. I didn't. I was about to lose ground in a spectacular way. One moment we were eight. Then we were seven. The older children's natural radar had guided them round the approaching hazard. The youngest, the rawest recruit, didn't have the technology and plunged headlong into the rawest pickle he had so far encountered in his few short years. The pity of war became the cess-pity of war. It is to the eternal credit of the magnificent seven that they paused to retrieve their stricken comrade. It was said the sound of the 'gloop' as they pulled him out could be heard in Luton.

The third great escape is a sorry tale of pure greed. If you have a queasy tummy, my advice is to skip this bit. I speak from authority. I have a queasy tummy and it dates precisely from this episode. Something else must be said before we go on. You know how these days it is all the rage to do genealogies or whatever you call them. You simply go online, push a few buttons, and all your forebears shuffle out like that banged-up gang from Fidelio. Well, in this case, we don't want to find out. We could unmask the perpetrator of the horror that befell me, but we won't. Let all stones remain unturned.

Those of you who have been following the plot closely will have noted I said I was the smallest child. Not quite true. There was also a baby on the payroll, at the crawling stage. We had little in common and our paths rarely crossed. It is that child's anonymity we must preserve. Hunger of course comes into it. One day, when the sweet airs of summer were upon the heath, I found myself alone in the front room of the cottage. The other residents were outside doubtless engaged in fragrant pursuits on grassy banks 'where the wild thyme grows'. It was then that I saw it, lying there on the floor, the 'chiefest jewel' in all the world, a Malteser. Maltesers, I should explain, are sweets, a confection, candy as the Americans say. They're round, roughly the size of a big marble, with a crunchy, biscuity centre covered with milk chocolate. I loved them. I loved them even more because sweets were rationed. They were the rarest of rare treats. And there, on the floor, on the well-worn lino, was a prime specimen. The joy, the exultation, the golden luck. But in a household of ten or more children you don't waste time. You have to be quick, if you're not, you get nothing. I swooped like a gannet. I never gave a thought to where the sweet might have come from. I completely forgot we had a one-year-old crawler amongst us. And, anyway, what did I know of infant digestive systems. But living in the country, as I now did, I had learned something about rabbit's habits. I knew the sort of thing they left behind.

Now I don't want you to get ahead of me here, though come to think of it, I wish you had at the time. Let me simply record I claimed the trophy for my own.

It was no Malteser. It looked like a Malteser. It weighed in as a Malteser might. But it was as far from being a Malteser as any object of its volume, displacement and colouring could be.

I spat it out! Spat! That's rich! You remember when the bomb blew in the kitchen window? Well, the force of my expectoration was easily equal to that. This was weapons grade spitting. The spat missile exited the cottage, then Hertfordshire, then gravity, and probably became the first brown hole in space. The young lungs never fully recovered from the effort involved. Mouthwash sales in the district rose dramatically. I've never before told a soul about this event. Please respect my confidence in this as in other delicate family matters.

I will conclude these, the first of my bucolic adventures, by reporting that except when stricken with I-want-my-Mum-itis, my stay in Kinsbourne Green, near Harpenden, Herts, was a blissfully happy time. But it was also the place where I first went to school and was beaten up by a kid called Jack who I hope is dead.

Chapter IX
The chain gang.

At what point I was repatriated to London, I don't know. I do know another school awaited, and this beggars belief, it was another nunnery! The Marist Convent in Fulham Road. What was with my Mum? I loved her yet she kept selling me into slavery, handing me over to the enemy at every opportunity. I hope she got a good price. At opening time on day one there was a dreadful screaming, shouting, kicking tantrum under the school's stone portal as I fought against going in. A bus driver on the Number 14 route slowed to watch, while the conductor probably took bets on the outcome. It was no contest. I was manhandled - womanhandled - into school. The bus moved on and the gates of doom clanged shut behind me. Marg was riding shotgun as usual to ease the pain. But it was Wealdstone all over again. Squadrons of Nazguls with their ebony bead chains and iron crosses circled. I was older now and though not streetwise, I was becoming convent wise.

Rule number one, stand still and check out the place for cesspits. Rule two, any signs of Friesians? If all clear, hold Margaret's hand and edge forward. I could hold a sister's hand with impunity because, needless to say, I was the only boy in the place, and needless to say again, I was still too young for this to matter. But the authorities always get you in the end. There's always a come on, a sugared pill, an enticer to make you feel at home. And you always fall for it. In this case it was the most unlikely thing that caught me off guard. A roundabout. Not a traffic roundabout, a fairground roundabout. A big proper, heavy iron roundabout, black as your hat, with a wide running board, slatted wooden seating and scaffold-size grab bars radiating from the centre.

'Would little Jimmy like a ride?'

Yes, little Jimmy would.

'Up we get then, there we are, hold tight now, round we go, round and round the mulberry bush … '

Little Jimmy sat there in the timeless right angle of childhood. Little body upright, little legs straight out, little shoes pointing upwards like serifs to his shins, little hand trustingly holding the scaffold bar. They'd got him now. Under the motive power of three Nazguls, middle distance runners all, the machine gathered pace. This was fine. The Nazguls loved this. They raced around whooping, their ebony bead chains whirring. Just before we reached the sound barrier they let go.

Little Jimmy, his curls flattened by the gale and his eyes bulging with centrifugal force, flashed past the onlookers at cinematographic projector speed. The laws of physics determined what happened next. At some point the momentum of spin overcame gravity and friction let go its hold on his trousers. He too, let go, parting company with his new seat of learning and setting off in an easterly direction like a shell from a howitzer. He didn't go far of course. The nearby brick wall stopped him. It didn't just stop him, it flattened him. The friable surface of the bricks clung to clothing and flesh and abraded him as he slid to the ground with a whimper. This confirmed my early doubts. Education might not be all plain sailing.

This reintroduction to school took place under the boughs of a mighty oak, or was it a spreading chestnut, or a beech, or a plane? A tree so great in girth its roots had pushed up the very tarmac of the playground itself. It had looked down, shaded me in my distress, but done nothing to help. I love trees, but I sometimes think they could be a bit more proactive.

The grounds of the Marist Convent had a further mantrap in store for unwary first-years. This was another ha-ha! I should explain that the playground at the Kinsbourne Green school was one big ha-ha! That is, in the field or common ground adjoining the tiny school building, a squarish sunken area with sloping grassy banks served as the place for our playtime frolics. It was upon one of these banks 'where the wild thyme etcetera, etcetera' that the villainous Jack indulged in one of his playtime frolics and duffed me up. I hope he's still dead. Because of this, I had returned to London with no great love for 45^0 angled grass slopes in summertime or winter. Now it so happened the architect who built the Marist Convent, decided to site the building on its foundation, with a concrete apron around the foot, complete with horizontal iron drainage grilles. He then set the whole edifice deep within a pit complete with 45^0 angled grass slopes. Ha, bloody, ha! Thanks to him, it was not long after the surgeons had signed off my roundabout wounds, that I caught their eye again. It was playtime. I was racing about in 'that ecstatic gallop only childhood knows' when I came across the sunken scenery. Surprisingly for one so young, I didn't lose my head, just my feet. Down we went.

Are you familiar with the industrial process for making potato crisps? No? Well, from the potato's point of view, things are similar to the fate of a hard-boiled egg when it meets a hard-boiled egg slicer. The wires come down, the severed parts of the egg part company and the whole falls neatly apart.

Now imagine tobogganing on your knees, out of control, in your short trousers with your bare, bulgy kneecaps leading the way. At the base of the slope are the blades of a drainage grille. The result does not make you feel chipper but it makes your knees look like they've been through a chipper. There was a song of the time:

'Your knee bone's connected to your thigh bone … '

It ain't necessarily so. If I had been older, I would have been a broken man. As it was, I was a broken child. If asked, I could have posed for one of the bloodfest paintings hanging round the walls. This scrape was even more tiresome than when they'd used me as a wrecking ball on their wall. The pain was equal, but the inconvenience greater because knees played a big part in Marist life. You spent half your days on them. They were very keen on kneeling. They favoured a down on one knee, duck-and-dive affair, an early form of the bunny dip. Without your knees, you were destined to play for the reserves for the foreseeable future.

What happened next was worse. Before he could make any friends - or a recovery - he was yet again transferred. Packed with little learning and many poultices, he was sent to yet another school. Presumably this was to teach him a lesson. By now the prospect of some straightforward chalk-and-blackboard teaching was appealing. Life's lessons so far had involved the loss of too many bodily fluids. He longed for peaceful academic instruction. But he remained cautious and wary. So he was pleased when he arrived at the new school to be asked a proper, grown up question.

'Why the tin bath?'

Chapter X
Cacky.

The initials of my mother's name, Cecilia Ann Kelso, CAK, gave Uncle Reg another opportunity to use his word skills. 'Cacky', he would call her from time to time. Understandably, she didn't like it. It caused big friction. To be fair, Uncle Reg didn't use the word too much. 'Cissie' was his chosen label of endearment.

To me, Mum was always just Mum. I don't, to my shame, know where she was born. I do know she was born in 1896, to a military family, the Millards. Her father, Grandad Millard, was a military tailor. The family, following the ways of army life, travelled. She had lived in South Africa. Could this have been because of the Boer Wars? The timing would be about right although she would only have been a five or six-year old. The wars were fought between the British and the descendants of the Dutch settlers. The Boers' leader was none other than Paul Kruger, my chum from my history lesson. I doubt though if he and Mum knew each other. He probably didn't even know Grandad. Come to think of it, if I'd realized Mum was in South Africa at the time, I could have mentioned her in my homework, to add a bit of local colour, a touch of human interest.

With Grandad still tailoring away, the family moved to India. There is a chance they were in India first and then moved to South Africa. In fact, I nearly found out the true sequence of events, by a fluke.

Decades later, when my mother was in her decline, in a home for the elderly, I would regularly visit her on Friday evenings. Once the pleasantries were over, there was little to talk about. The visits became mind-numbingly tedious. Then I had the idea of pretending to be a journalist interviewing a celebrity. Tongue in cheek, I produced a pencil and notepad and started asking pertinent and impertinent questions. As you'd expect, enquiries about yesterday, last week, or last month drew a predictable blank. But the age-old memories were all there. At first to my delight, then to my increasing unease, from the torpor of decline stepped out the little curly-haired girl she had once been. It was unbearably sad and upsetting. Of my own volition, I had introduced myself to a complete stranger, a person, a child I'd never met. Of course the little girl remembered South Africa and India.

'And do you know, when we sailed to India we went on the same liner as the one we sailed to South Africa on.'

Her voice was childlike and vigorous. The joy of that long ago coincidence brought unbidden tears of pleasure to her face.

I couldn't go on. Today I can't look at what I wrote at the time. My innocent, playful Friday evening ploy I came to see as intrusive, verging on the abusive. I remembered how uneasy I'd felt when I read of Sigmund Freud psychoanalysing his youngest daughter, prying into the secrets of her sex life, and demonstrating his own lack of ordinary psychological insight. And here was I ventriloquising a child back to life. I never did it again. Another word for mind-numbing tediousness is peace.

Mum didn't get a lot of peace even when the Millards returned to England - perhaps to Colchester? Cecilia was one of how many children? Kit, Winnie, Ethel, Uncle Ed, was it five, including her? When they were back in the old country there was a short straw to be drawn. Although her Dad had no doubt been stitching away diligently, pickings were lean. There wasn't enough money. The family therefore did what families often did in those days. They slung one out of the nest. The one they chose to sling was Mum. Why she was chosen? Was she the oldest, the youngest, the most capable, I don't know. She certainly had the one necessary qualification to be given the heave-ho, namely she was a girl. She could be put into service. Not the armed services, the skivvying service, the house-maiding drudgery, below stairs, living in, working for the nobs of nob hill. Not slavery, not owned, not indentured, nothing. She joined the ranks of the servile, status-less persons. She felt about it much as I did when she got me to the nunnery. She didn't like it. She did not like the fact her family had given her the elbow. That hurt never left her. She was a forgiving soul and would later treat them with a generosity they had been forced to deny her. She knew they didn't deserve it. So did they. Kindness can be a sweet revenge.

Do you know Chelsea? The embankment? Between Albert and Chelsea bridges, beautiful part of the world, ruined like everywhere else by traffic, but beautiful none the less. Magnificent houses, elegant gardens, hanging baskets of flowers, even the street furniture is handsome, great anchored-down Swan iron benches. Walk along from Albert Bridge to the junction with Royal Hospital Road. Go a little way past, stop, turn and look back at the houses to your left. High up, behind one of those tiny windows was the room in which Mum served out her servility. After she became tenant of The Rising Sun, and one of the first women licensees in the country, she would sometimes on her afternoon off, walk to that spot and sit and look up at the window. She took me there once and pointed it out. Later, in another lifetime, I sat there on my own, reflecting on the fact that, hanging in a house a few doors along, was a painting of mine, bought from that year's Royal Academy Summer Exhibition. Mum would have liked that. She may have been a bit sniffy about the subject matter of the painting, but she would have enjoyed the moment.

So how did the serving wench escape from the high window? She didn't jump and she didn't escape alone. Liberation for her, and millions of other put upon women all over the world, came from the arrival of war.

'Oh, oh, oh, what a lovely war'.

Thank God for that Mum may have said. 'Half the seed of Europe' was about to be wiped out, but most of the females of the species would come through bereaved but otherwise unscathed.

Gunnery was what got her out, munitions. She helped build the shells that fed the 'monstrous anger of the guns'. Where she juggled the gelignite, I do not know. But it wasn't in that tiny room, behind that high window, overlooking the Thames, and that was the important thing. Maybe she was over at Woolwich Arsenal, in Old Man Kelso country. I've no idea. She must have been good at bomb making - there'd be much demand for her services today - because she was made a foreman woman. This promotion, her war record, and one other natural attribute, led to further commercial triumphs.

Cecilia Ann Millard had a good speaking voice. It was well modulated, cultured, pleasant on the ear. Cultured tones, dulcet tones, they were called. After she gave up bombing, presumably when peace broke out, her voice enabled her to get a job as a telephone operator. Quaint though it may seem now, this carried a certain social cachet. I should explain that in that era, when you used the telephone, you spoke to a human being. The Post Office, who ran the scam, did not sully their apparatus with unschooled Eliza Doolittles. There were strict rules and regulations including tuition on voice production almost like a stage school. For telephone operators a decent, well-mannered speaking voice was desirable, it wasn't the hindrance it is today. It was a genuine asset. Silly old Billys weren't they.

Mum climbed to even dizzier heights. The highest rung of the operator's ladder was to work on the international exchange. That was the gold standard and Mum made it. What a time it must have been. Whenever you picked up the phone, you received pronunciation.

Chapter XI
Where there's a will.

My mother was perfect. She was also Irish, although I was never aware of it. She had no hint of an accent. I doubt if she could have worked as an international telephonist if she'd had one. Her singing might have given me a clue. Mum sang in a pleasant, unselfconscious way as she went about her work. It was guileless and charming, a sunny soundtrack to her days. She sang quietly, without thinking, in a way unthinkable today where song is unnatural, manufactured, amplified, priced, bought, sold, copyrighted, every utterance an audition. Not back then. Come rain or shine, Mum would sing the airs of old.

Hitler would download his high explosives. Mum would sing.

'O, Danny Boy, … ' KER-WHOOMPH! ' … The pipes, the pipes are calling you … ' KER-KRRRASH! ' … From glen to glen … ' KERR-WALLOP! ' … and down the mountain side … ' KER-KRRRUNCH!

Her only amplifier, the occasional tin bath, Mum sang on through the storm, she walked on through the rain, and she'll never walk alone.

Her mother, Mary, I regret may have to. I know nothing about Mary or that side of the family. What I need is a crane's foot. The crane's foot in French, so I read on the back of a corn flakes packet, is pied de grue. This has mangled itself into our word pedigree, because the mark used in genealogies to denote succession, looks like a crane's footprint. Regrettably not many of my lot have left prints in the sands of time. The more I write, the more I realize I don't know who's who, what's what, or when was when. We don't have a family mausoleum; we have a family Bermuda triangle.

I think everyone should be encouraged at school to write their family history. That's my theory of relativity. It would add to the nation's archive and cause immense mischief. I can give you chapter and verse about Paul Kruger, but what good is that when I'm seeking Grandma Mary? And if I know nothing about Mary, what about the black hole that is my knowledge of the Kelsos?

I think it was on another cereal pack I read:

'If you stand with your parents behind you, one each side, each with a hand on your shoulder; and behind them stand their parents and so on, you don't have to go back many rows and you have an impossibly large number, bigger than the total of all the people who have ever lived.'

This is because we all marry cousins, a tad removed maybe, but cousins none the less. The gaps in chronology and individual histories of my family exceed the parts I can recall. It doesn't mean that's all there is - or was - but it's all I have to go on. I'm as much defined by ignorance as knowledge.

So, amid the loved ones the neglected ones.

Another soul, like Mary, whom I never met, was my paternal grandmother. All I know is the fate that befell her and which keeps her story fresh in mind. She had a son who bore the same name as me, James Philip Kelso. He died during the First World War, aged 21. He fell victim to a 'flu epidemic two weeks after he joined the army. He was stationed at Woolwich Arsenal. On hearing of his death, his mother stopped speaking. Because of her silence, she was eventually committed to an institution, maybe a mental home. Her family visited regularly. For many mute years this went on. Then on one visit they found she had been moved to a new ward. They, in their usual one-sided, talking-among-themselves sort of way, asked how she liked her new surroundings. She replied:

'I was perfectly all right where I was.'

She never spoke again and died, in the same home, years later. For years I had a military medal, struck in her son's honour, bearing his name - my name - in a drawer. It's not there now. It's currently filed under mislaid.

You could by now be wondering why I don't bother to find the missing pieces of the family jigsaw Why the disinclination, the disinterest? Could it be distaste perhaps? You see there's still the matter of the will. Hearsay again, but it's all I have. When my father managed the Grove Tavern in Hammersmith, working for Old Man Kelso, there was already ill will between Mum and the Old Man. Presumably the cause was because he'd forced Dad into the trade. Whatever it was, the dislike was there. So much so, when Mum would go to meet Dad, she'd wait outside the pub until after closing time, refusing to go in. She'd wait until he'd come out to walk home together to their flat in Burnfoot Avenue. I can't imagine Hammersmith Grove at closing time in the 1930s was any less threatening for a young woman alone than it is today, in our own vodka and vomit times. But she wouldn't go in.

'Once,' she told me, 'the Old Man himself came out into the street and begged me to, but I said no.'

Then came the move to the Sun, a move she detested. Imagine that detestation. You can't abide your in-laws and then you have to move in with them. To live under the same roof, taking with you all the chattels you'd brought from the home you loved. It must have been ghastly. And it got worse.

Not long afterwards, Old Man Kelso died. He had a second wife who, of course, was also living there. Ten weeks after his death she, though a much younger woman, also died. I state these facts baldly with no disrespect. I simply know nothing more about these deaths. But I do know what they meant. Old Man Kelso's wealth was now up for grabs. His fictional fortune was on the market. There followed the descent of the siblings. Dad's brothers and sisters who had managed to not be around, Mum said, when help was needed.

'Like vultures they were,' Mum said.

'I had to count out every item in the house into piles. Everything right down to the pillow cases, everything including our own possessions we'd brought to the Sun. Everything in that household was fair game for the vulture pack.'

Her anger at this unfairness would flare as she recalled it. The vultures' disbelief that the Old Man hadn't left a hidden hoard of treasure led to disappointment. Off they went clutching their pillowcases and bitterness.

'Of course, he didn't leave a fortune,' Mum said. 'He spent the money, £10 a day every day for years! I saw it with my own eyes!'

Years later, long after my Dad's death, there was some rapprochement. Mum, as usual, would be what she ever was by nature, courteous, polite, even generous to them. Indeed, she may have forgiven them.

But she never forgot.

Chapter XII
The remains of helmet.

Mum never forgot the vultures. Did she have a good memory? Perhaps. It seems to me the task of doing the family forgetting has fallen to me. The amount I can't recall far outweighs what I can.

Take Mum's father, the journeyman tailor, Grandpa Millard. How little I know of him. His retirement was spent living alone in a cottage in Colchester, up the hill from St Botolph's railway station, opposite the great wall of the military barracks, turn in alongside the Cambridge pub, down a narrow lane and at the far end of the cul-de-sac, there it is on the right, you can't miss it.

It is only by furrowing the brow have I recalled his name: Harry, or maybe Henry. He lived alone with twelve giant spiders. He visited the Sun from time to time in my early years but left no trace. We have to fast-forward to pick up his spoor. We were taken occasionally on holiday to stay with him and I loved it. For a start we went by train, steam train, from Liverpool Street, ter-tum, ter-tum, der-dun, der-dun.

'Caution,' read the notice, 'bye law pursuant to the Railways Act of 1892 do not lean out of the window while the train is in motion!' Gerroff! That's the best time. Yank down the leather strap window, head out, neck straining, sucking in the smoke, swallowing the soot, savouring the smell, waiting for the oncoming Flying Scotsman to part your hair. All eyes out to see who could first spot, on the skyline, Colchester's distinctive water tower. This was, arguably, as near perfect as things have ever got, especially if Dud was there a well. By this time, I'd acquired a best friend, Dudley. Happily, he was sometimes taken on these holiday jaunts, cheering me up no end for he too had been bitten by the steam bug in early life.

He lived a little way along Fulham Road from the Sun, just opposite the Britannia pub. His home became almost a home-from-home for me. It was a large detached house on four floors, set in a big garden with, at the back, a huge glass-roofed workshop. It has all gone now, of course, destroyed. The workshop was a working and busy foundry, a sculptor's foundry. There were shelves upon shelves of busts and figurines, row after row of standing statues, their blind eyes aloof and strange. I was intrigued by them, then and now. I'd love to have known more about it but was too young to ask. Dudley's parents were kindness itself to me and though he and I went to different schools, we spent hours up in their living room on the top floor, drawing and listening to the American Forces Network - was the disc-jockey Rex Stewart? - corrupting us with Stan Kenton and other bands, the music only interrupted by the occasional bulletin: '... and now the news brought to you by the wires of AP, UP and INS...' This was exciting and adventurous.

What did we draw? What do you mean what did we draw? Da-boing! of course. Da-boing! was a character we'd invented and, hot-diggity-dog, was he quick. He spent his days hurtling from place to place at supersonic speed. Never has a special agent been followed by so many blur marks. When not blurring from foot to foot, Da-boing! travelled in the greatest of great style, greater than the greatest style you can imagine. His steeds were none other than his fleet of fin-fendered, streamlined hymns to the goddess chromium, the awesome Buicks, Pontiacs, Studebakers, Oldsmobiles and - hold that drool, Cadillacs - the same superlative vehicles that constricted the hearts and throats of all rightly brought up minors in that enlightened era. These cars were so wonderful we simply had to steal them mentally.

In the Michelin building on the corner of Fulham Road and Sloane Avenue there was a showroom, a showcase, a shrine to be knelt before, devoted to the display and sale of the American dream, the great American automobile. It drew us like a beacon. We'd ride there on our bikes and if we were lucky the salesmen would perhaps be moving vehicles. The great glass doors would part and the vast monsters would emerge, their scornful whitewall tyres squealing imperiously on the mean streets of Kensington. We would stand at a respectful distance, leaning on our crossbars and watch, gazing longingly at the gleaming polish, enviously eyeing the bench seats and the magic of the great spaceship fins. Then we'd submit our claims. We had a simple method of claiming ownership. Whoever saw one of these streamliners first had to bag it for their own by bellowing:

'Baggsie, baggsie, all mine, all mine!'

Whoever shouted out first, the treasure was his. No down payments, no hire purchase, no contract hire, no dodgy leasing. One 'baggsie, all mine!' and it was yours forever and always. A simple system with much to recommend it. Didn't it lead to conflict, simultaneous shoutings, competing claims? Rarely. Even if you did spy one at the same time, one or other of you was always halfway through a doughnut or some other gobstopper. Muffled claims didn't count. You couldn't submit them to the DVLA. These car sightings took place all over the extent of our cycling range, a territory limited only by the requirement to be home by teatime.

When we were loosed into Grandpa's Essex, we were starved of such delights. We had to be content with other games. Grandad was by then a large, sedentary soul. He sat in his armchair all day long, smoking his pipe. He wore his bowler hat at all times, including indoors. His whole cottage seemed to smoke a pipe. I think even his giant spiders may have been on the Old Holborn. The cottage was blue with pipe fumes. I liked the sweet, cloying smell.

The window of our bedroom in the cottage overlooked a small mews of lockup garages. This was the local Brooke Bond Tea depot. Their silent, bright red electric vans set out from there each morning to distribute the 'vital oolong' to the caffeine-starved folk gasping in the nearby terraces. I loved to look down on the workers toiling at their labours, lifting and loading, exchanging cheery morning pleasantries with their fellows before setting off on their rounds. How great it must be to be grown up.

On the opposite wall of our bedroom lived the arachnids *(whopperus, whopperus)*. The wall was damp; some of the wallpaper had sagged and bulged into bubbles. Behind these lived the eight-legged. At night when we lay in our beds, out they would come. Such was the acoustic configuration of the arrangement, when one of the monsters walked over a bubble you could hear its footsteps, pit-pat, pit-pat, multiplied by eight. It was around this time I learnt to spell the word harrowing. I never slept easy, I just lay there, ears alert for the dreaded pit-a-pats and praying for the merry Brooke

Bonders to arrive. The waking nightmare was so great on one occasion we decided a cull was the only solution. 'If you want to live and thrive let a spider run alive.' Yes we know that, but special dispensation, please. It took thirteen long-range shots, turn and turn about, using a stout elastic band to kill one of the brutes. The scuttling horror of this event left its mark. We were too spooked even to lug the guts and throw them out of the window. We only did this deed once. We left the rest of the colony alone, hoping they'd feel the same way about us. Ever since, I've been kindness itself to the whole genus, living-and-let-living to the utmost degree. I even own a spider plant as part of my rehab.

Further along the lane beyond Grandpa's cottage at the end of the cul de sac, behind the military church, was an area of private waste ground the size of a football pitch. The only building on the scene, apart from the back of the lapboard church, was a long mournful, dilapidated workshop stretching the length of one touchline.

This was the realm of Mr Gurney, a friend of Grandad's. He would let us play in the rubble of undergrowth and overgrowth, his only proviso being don't get in among his runner beans. I don't know what career he had followed in his early professional days, but whatever he did now, he did it in the workshop wearing a dark suit, jacket off, waistcoat on, with a neat collar and tie. His workshop contained one item of lung-bursting excitement, a souvenir Mr Gurney had brought back from the First World War.

A German tin helmet.

This was no tin bath to be worn on your head. This was the real thing, the arrogant iron of war, the headgear of some luckless long-gone Teuton. We gasped even to touch it. Despite my tender age, the sight of it took me back to an even tenderer age when I had first confronted cold steel, eye-to-eye. This was in the Sun and I had almost fallen to my doom from the top of a wardrobe as a result.

Scary.

Chapter XIII
'Twas in another lifetime ... '

Scary, indeed. And things don't get much scarier than when you have, aged four, climbed to the top of your mother's wardrobe and on looking down you realise there's no way to climb back. The chasm yawns. Four years old! These days, when I have to be carbon dated to get a passport, it seems quaint to think that ages can be counted in single figures. The most sophisticated attitude to the ageing process came to me after I had children of my own. One school fête day, having been saddled with the pony rides job, I was leading the bored pony round the field for the hundredth time. A nipper was on board, clutching the reins, wobbling limply in the wind.

'What's your name?' I said disinterestedly.

'Joe,' he said.

'How old are you? I said.

'I don't know,' he said.

Even the pony gave a hoarse laugh.

So there I was, up on the furniture. The wardrobe was elaborately veneered wood, with a full-length mirrored door and a deep drawer full width across the bottom. I'd already rifled through the drawer and found no treasures. Now, as I knelt up top, I could feel the plywood top giving dangerously under my weight. But, you know what it's like, while you're up there, 'silent, upon a peak in Darien', you might as well have a peek around. There was the usual top-of-cupboard lumber, a brace of hats, a tasselled lampshade that had seen better days, an old basket, bits of this, bits of that, and a bundle of something wrapped in cloth, tied with string. A weighty bundle to small hands. Odd shape, too, not square, not round, just odd. Better take a look, you can't be sure when you'll be passing this way again. Untie string. Unwrap cloth. More cloth. Unwrap more cloth. A leather case, odd tapering shape. Undo buckle, open flap at one end. Inside, paper, stiff paper, yellowish almost brown. Greaseproof paper. Smell of oil in the air. Unwrap carefully, slowly. And there it was, its menace finally revealed to the wide-eyed child. A Webley service revolver, cleaned, oiled and in perfect working order. Small hearts could thud no faster; small jaws could drop no further.

Was it loaded? Of course it was loaded! It was freighted with the tears of Ypres and the mud of Flanders. The cold metal sweated in the unaccustomed air. It wasn't sweating as much as its finder. Like thunder the sound effects came

72

drumming in his ears ... the cries and battle hymns of the world's republics ... 'aux armes, citoyen!' ... 'come the four corners of the world in arms!' ... 'to me lads, to me!' ... 'from the halls of Montezuma, to the shores of Tripoli!' ... 'red leader, red leader! angels one five!' ... 'Shane, come back Shane!' ... 'up periscope, fire number one!' ... 'we shall fight on the beaches' ... 'we shall never surrender'.

It's fair to say - except for the sight of the Royal Scot taking refreshment at full speed from the water troughs outside Watford Junction - the top of the wardrobe find remained the apogee of my existence until the onset of puberty. As you would expect, the discovery of this grim ordnance made a profound impact upon the growing child. But it was nothing compared to the profound impact made by the growing child when he walked into the kitchen where the family was having lunch and, pointing the shooter, said:

'Hands up, all those who want to see what I've found.'

Details are sketchy but I recall an air of excitement. No mishap ensued. At the hastily called disarmament conference negotiations were successfully concluded and I never saw the piece again. I would later have a vision of what might have been the result of this unwitting prank, but we'll come to that in a moment.

The kitchen in the Sun was furnished with one or two excessively good don't-touch-that toys. One was the icebox that

73

served as a fridge. This was a cabinet with a close fitting lid that shut out the air and heat. The box was lined with fluted corrugated sheeting, very thermally efficient. A solid block of ice, the size of a small suitcase provided the cooling. The iceman cometh once a week on his horse-drawn cart. The size of block was specified and, with the aid of giant iron callipers, it was carried upstairs on strong shoulders covered with protective hessian sacking. The ice was loaded downwards into the slot aperture, which occupied about one-third of the volume of the total. The other two-thirds were for the victuals. And there we were, the cool kids on the block, chilled out for another week. The icebox naturally contained treats, ice cream and so on. There was an embargo in place of course, and rigidly enforced. I raided the cabinet from time to time, but never managed to fulfil my dream. This was to hide inside it and spring out, like Kathy Seldon from her cake in Singin' in the Rain, when the lid was next lifted. This would definitely have put some colour into Mum's cheeks. The child did not consider what it might have done to Dora's bloomers. The more likely scenario was of someone discovering the remains of me in the icebox, grinning up at them, frozen white.

But it was not to be.

I did however once manage to get inside the dumb waiter. This was a lift with rope pulleys, by which food was lowered from kitchen to bar and back up with the dirty plates. It was a simple, highly effective arrangement, sturdily designed and built with counterweights to take say, half a dozen plates of meat-and-two-veg, all well within prevailing health and safety margins. These regulations did not cover the carriage of four-year olds during opening hours.

There were two shelves, a floor so to speak, and a removable mid-shelf. It is an iron rule among four-year olds; if things can be removed they must be, and not put back, but left lying around at random. The dimensions of the lift in old money were, I'd guess, 30″ high by 20″ wide by 20″ deep. Now what does the average, not too supple, four-year-old fold up into, volumetrically speaking? Well, speaking from my own experience, just over 30″x 20″x 20″.

One quiet afternoon I set out on my own private journey to the centre of the earth. The lift had a small shelf in front of it. Once on the shelf the child, clutching the thick pulley rope tight in one hand, could slide rear-end first into the capsule. A severe neck bend was required to insert the head in above the tail. Twist, squirm, squeeze, wriggle, rotate, and enter the zone. It was quite a surprising thing to learn about dumb waiters. They're not as dumb as you think. They have a point of criticality. This revealed itself in that minutest of moments, that nanosecond when the amount of weight in the waiter, exceeded the avoirdupois of the remaining limbs being supported by the shelf. Gravitationally speaking, the difference between security and insecurity is small. My cereal packs tell me there is, as yet, no experimental evidence for the existence of the postulated graviton particle. Huh! It not only exists, I know where it lives. And it took only one to tip the balance. The plummet began. As it did so a thought, among other things, struck me. It's one thing to gradually solidify in an ice box while licking your favourite ice cream, but quite another to hurtle into a saloon bar in a foetal position with the skin burned off your hands from trying to apply the brakes. It was too late. We fell 'full fathoms five' - or that was what it felt like - in reality it was only twelve inches or so before we jammed. We were saved by our own sticking out appendages including part of the head. Houston had yet to be built but it already had a problem. Let's not dwell on this. The exit was prolonged and inelegant. Shortly after it had been accomplished an anonymous adult entered the room. Seeing the warped and reddened infant tottering in small circles, bent like a paper clip, it enquired:

'What have you been up to?'

'Nothing.'

I didn't think of a better reply until the spring of 1959 after reading The Hunchback of Notre Dame.

But back to our vision of what might have been with the Webley.

Lifts and iceboxes aside, our meals, with the exception a few special Christmas-type events, we're taken in the kitchen. Mum was a superb cook of the sliced hard-boiled egg on a bed of lettuce with Heinz salad cream variety. Her roast potatoes and succulent chickens cause noses to twitch in anticipation even unto the 21st century. This day, then, we were cheerily at the trough as usual, the child now eight or nine years old, all intent on our own doings. Uncle Reg sat to my right in front of the icebox. Mum to my left in front of the oven, Marg, if she was there, would have been opposite me. I can't remember if she was or not. Perhaps memory has shut her off to protect her from the stupendous events that followed.

Our table was always furnished with proprietary condiments, brown sauce, tomato sauce, the usual brands. Nose deep in my comic, I reached for my choice of the day. In those days, sauces were in bottles, none of your squeezy plastic nozzles squirting out itsy-bitsy globules. No, we had proper full-throated hygienic glass. My chosen condiment was the tomato variety, the one that is viscous and takes a long time to pour. It's well worth the wait, but childhood is an impatient time. I gave the bottle a monster shake. Now it just so happened someone, and I swear it was not me m'Lud, had left the top off. The viscosity of the contents was as nothing to the violence of the shake. The wide-mouthed aperture allowed a large portion of the enclosed to leave the bottle in the direction of the icebox. It would have covered it completely if Uncle Reg hadn't been in the way. The broadside took him square in the shirtfront except for several fluid ounces that landed smack in the kisser. I'm surprised you didn't hear the uproar that followed, or perhaps you did. It was so loud I looked up in alarm from my comic. The words Quentin Tarantino didn't spring to mind. Not then.

What was springing to life was the table, several chairs, numerous roundels of hard-boiled eggs and He's-Not-Your-Real-Father-You-Know. Uncle Reg seemed to have expanded in the excitement. He was a big man to begin with, still in his prime, but not still in his seat. He was well used to the pursuit and upending of right-wingers of international standing. This was not the occasion when he slung me downstairs, but the motivation level was similar.

All I had on my side was the wriggle factor. There followed a chase over difficult country, round and round the roof garden, up and over box mattresses, under beds, in and out of cupboards, up and down stairs. During these revels I gained the impression that if the long-gone Webley had come to hand Uncle Reg may have abdicated his avuncular duties and risked the wrath of the constabulary.

In the distance I could I could hear the United Nations of Mum and other spectators attracted by the commotion, yelling 'accidents can happen'. To which He's-Not-Your-Real-Father-You-Know replied with a roar that one was about to.

Towards evening we found Dur-Dur trembling on top of the wardrobe where the original offence had taken place years before. Three days later Mickey the cat came home of its own accord, so that was good. As to what brand of ketchup, oh no. I must protect my sauces.

Chapter XIV
The lull before the lull.

For a brief period the air raids ceased. The sirens were silent. The tin baths lay unused. But not all the fun went out of life. This gave us more time to play with our trains. This was when I fell under the spell of steam. I wasn't alone: Jimmy Bledlow, Johnny Hunt, Derek Large and Dudley, of course, we were all bewitched. It wasn't only the spell we fell under. There were ample opportunities for serious injury.

Our playground was Wandon Road, a turning by the Stamford Arms. Today it's a wasteland of homes and other rubbish. Back then it was empty thoroughfare, running down from Fulham Road before sweeping up to join New King's Road opposite the Nell Gwynne pub. It was a huge tarmacadam'd, car free area. On one side stood a row of terraced cottages, in one of which lived Jimmy Bledlow.

How we envied him.

Opposite his front door, a mere hundred paces away, stood the abandoned and derelict Fulham and Chelsea railway station. The footprint of the building was aitch-shaped. The two wings were joined in the middle by a set back booking hall with a canopied forecourt. On each side ran a corrugated, cruelly pointed iron fence, with barbed wire above. This marked the rear of the station's platform.

If, at night, you stood on the platform with your back to the fence and walked a few paces forward you'd pitch head first over the edge on to the rails. It was easily done. It was regularly done. The station's windows were boarded up. Under the forecourt's canopy the main doors were bolted and padlocked, never to open to the travelling public again. Note: not never to open again, simply not to the travelling public, a subtle and known-to-our-gang-only difference. Behind the doors was the booking hall with its ticket office window, the glass still fogged with the breath of a thousand forgotten third class returns. Opposite this, half-open doors lead to empty, echoing offices. There was no graffiti. This was due not only to the absence of the not-yet-invented spray can. It spoke of a higher-toned calibre of breaker-and-enterer. Not for us the tedious tagging, the repetitive standardised signing, dreary defacement, outstretched arms describing artless arcs, empty of invention.

There was one exception. On the bolted and padlocked double-doors was an official hand-painted message in large black letters. It invited us to Keep Out! The iron heel of authority lay heavy on the land. We took note but we didn't take notice. We weren't defacers or vandalisers. We were the keepers of the flame, the station wraiths who melted into the masonry. This was 'Baggsie all mine! All ours!' And all hours of day and night in those icy, smog-filled winters, it was ours alone.

We played two games: one was forgery, the other, terrorism.

To get on the platform we shinned up a telegraph pole and once over the fence, we were unseen. Two types of trains came through, freight trains and troop trains. There were no passenger trains. The troop trains were pulled by 2-6-0 locomotives - a type we called soldiers' engines. The troops would hang out of the windows and throw coins or sweets to us - or it may have been at us. The U.S. soldiers were the most generous, showering us with chewing gum and candy called Life Savers. If we got a good haul of sixpenny pieces - tanners - we'd put them on the line and wait for the next train to flatten them into the size of a shilling, worth double.

Mr Davis at the sweetshop may have had a gammy leg but he had eagle eyes. We never fooled him. Not surprising. Our 'shillings' were as thin as milk-bottle tops. Also our production methods were too hit and miss. The coins often vibrated off the rails. We needed to improve our quality control. One suggestion was for a volunteer to lie on the ground close to the sleepers and hold the coin in place with a stick until the wheels went over it.

Good thinking.

We decided to do a feasibility study. To the left of the platform, by the Fulham Road bridge was a set of signals. We didn't mess with signals. They were big and unpredictable. They went up and down without warning, like a parent's temper. But there was flat patch of ground just there, a niche, with a brick wall behind it that was suitable. On the appointed night, a three-man recce party settled down in the coal dust and oil sludge. We weren't foolhardy. Our faces were about six feet to the side and twelve inches above the rails. A safe distance from the action, you'll agree. We didn't have long to wait.

The train came. The train passed. The train ter-tum, ter-tummed into the distance.

The recce party did not emerge immediately. They remained for a while, unmoving - I'm tempted to say frozen but that is not the word - like figures in a Caravaggio painting. The tableau was lit by a small fire in Jimmy Bledlow's hair. Someone, his face rosy and moisturized by superheated steam, pricked a blister and put out the blaze. Then slowly - like the prisoners from Fidelio - out they came.

After that we gave up forgery and went back to terrorism.

Actually, terrorising is more accurate. We had worked out a way of scaring ourselves witless that was so successful we felt it unfair to keep it a secret. It cried out to be shared with others so they, in turn, could cry out.

It was all about dares. Dares were part of life.

The challenge was simple. I dare you to walk from one end of the deserted platform and back again, without running.

What could be easier?

In the cold light of day, nothing. In the coal black of night, it was different.

Factor in the often sub-zero temperatures, the cloaking darkness of a wartime blackout, the silence, the risk of being caught trespassing, the cavernous abyss of the empty ticket hall where who knows what tramps, derelicts or German spies might have taken refuge. Even the stout hearted shivered. Jimmy Springer was half way along the outward leg one night when the signalman's keys rattled in the fence door. There was a scuttling blur, some choked-off shouts followed at school register next morning by:

'J. Springer?

'Absent, Sir.'

It was soon after this that the Hortensia plot was hatched.

Hortensia - we called him that because he lived near Hortensia Road - was a nice enough kid, a 'decent sort of pig' as Uncle Reg used to say. We decided to test his mettle. This was a great honour for him. It showed we trusted him to keep our secret.

I should just mention something else here. This was the business of the khaki torch.

This torch had recently been lobbed from a train by some passing U.S. troops. The soon-to-be-singed J. Bledlow had collared it and claimed it for his own. We'd never seen anything like it. It was square sectioned and could shine white, red or green. Could the weaponry of war go further?

But back to the plot.

It was arranged that Bledlow - he was the bravest and, after all, he did have a torch - would go over the top at dusk and wait concealed in the ticket hall. We would meet the victim after nightfall and issue the dare. We'd then send Hortensia tiptoeing past the hall and our man within would moan 'Whoo-hoo!' in an owly voice.

The very thought of it sent our adrenaline surging.

Like D-day, it worked perfectly, though not without casualties. Unknown to even his close confederates, Bledlow kept a trick up his sleeve.

Hortensia arrived as arranged and under the cover of darkness we guided him up the pole. He was understandably nervous. This was his first trespass. We encouraged and reassured him with tales of many escapes from signalmen, guard dogs, railway police and other guardians of the peace. At last, slowly and with much trepidation, he set off along the platform and disappeared into the blackness.

We waited for the distant 'Whoo-hoo!' It didn't come. We waited an eternity.

Then it came.

Not the prearranged 'Whoo-hoo!' But a caterwauling howl of such despair mere words cannot express it. Mathematics alone can convey its awfulness:

$10^{aaarrrggh!}$

Even ten to the power of aaarrrgghh! is as nothing to the reality of Hortensia's song as he bulleted away into the night. One of his sisters later confided that he didn't begin to decelerate until he reached his aunt's house near Herne Hill.

No sooner had he flown than we saw the reason for his acceleration.

Coming slowly towards us along the platform, floating in mid air against the velvet black night was a gruesome disembodied green face. The countenance of our co-conspirator, Bledlow, J., was grisly enough in the kindly light of day. At night, lit from below, it was off the scale of awfulness. Once again the adrenaline surged. To keep the adrenaline company we too surged, going up the telegraph pole and blurring away past milk shop, greengrocer and confectioner, heading for hearth and homelands.

The U.S. standard issue khaki torch, held pointing upwards under the chin, lighting the features in ghostly green, helped secure great swathes of the western front for Allied forces.

For our part, other victims were subsequently recruited. They went down like flies.

As for Hortensia, he was never the same again. His shadow grew paler. He may even have become a Queens Park Rangers supporter.

Chapter XV
'A head half full of empty.'

'A head half full of empty' is how someone described their recall of childhood. That's what I have about Arundel where Uncle Ed and Aunt Thelma lived. Edward Millard was Mum's brother. The Millards were the educated wing of the pied de grue. Uncle Ed was headmaster of St Philip's Catholic Primary School - was he also Mayor of Arundel at one time? They and their children lived in a big house next to the school with a wonderful overgrown garden.

Learning and authority always impress me. This feeling may have started in Arundel. To this day I feel disrespectful referring to Uncle Ed as Uncle Ed even though that was what he was called. There was an aura about the place that inspired servility in me, no doubt well deserved. A glance from him and it was Pranks nil, Uncle Ed one. Not that these were prankish times. I was too young.

Were we evacuated there?

We certainly stayed for some time, though it may have been just a long school holiday. What I recall most is feeling cold, timid and missing Mum. That and brick arches under the school building leading out to a playground field.

Dukes, too, I remember Dukes. Arundel was, and probably still is, the manor of the Duke of Norfolk. This noble lived over the road from Uncle Ed, in a castle. His garden, I was told, extended to somewhere south of Yorkshire. Do I see a drawbridge and a moat? I think so, but I'm not certain.

I am certain the Duke figured a lot in conversation. He evidently took his Duking seriously and was much respected for it. He exerted considerable influence on the community and Uncle Ed's household. It was Duke this, Duke that. The Duke's coming, bustle bustle. The Duke's going, hustle hustle.

I never met His Grace. I don't think I ever set eyes on him, though Arundel was certainly the place I first met the male of the species, Nazgul.

The school had connections with The Cathedral of Our Lady and St Philip Howard, along the road. Instead of nuns, flocks of priests abounded. Like the female of the species, male Nazguls sported black frocks and chains of ebony beads with iron crosses on the end. Mercifully they didn't wear the headgear, the cowls. This made them less spooky. They differed from their sisterhood in that I never received a scowl from them. In fact during this whole period I was treated with kindness. Of course Marg was with me, riding shotgun, so I was in safe hands.

If not, I may have resorted to plan B. By now I could auto-induce ill symptoms sending my temperature to combustible levels. This unfailingly produced the desired effect; Mum would arrive. I wasn't happy at Arundel. I preferred the casual camaraderie of the tin bath. Arundel wasn't like that. So a belated thanks to everyone, but all I wanted to do was to go back to London and be bombed. So that's what we did.

Things brightened up on the Arundel front much later. One year, when the primrose of peace lay once more upon the land, we went there on holiday. Dudley was in tow so prospects were good. We weren't disappointed. We had an excellent time and, for a change, we weren't to blame. We did not instigate the disaster. We simply spectated and, truly, we didn't know the adults had it in them. Uncle Ed, Uncle Reg, Mum, the clergy, aunts, cousins, they put on a fine show for us.

Someone suggested a day's outing on the river, including a picnic. Arundel sits astride the tidal River Arun. Now - let me see - am I getting memories here of the Sea Scouts' boat being used? I think so. We were a large party, 12 or 15 even, including children, adults and priests. The day was beautiful. The boat was huge, as big and sturdy a rowing boat as I'd ever seen. She was moored on the offside of another craft. There was much clambering over and climbing down to get aboard. Then we were off, the adults rowing. The trick with tidal rivers is to go with the flow. Let the water do all the hard work and little rowing effort is needed. We drifted peaceably along amid summer's serenity. Steering was naught but a nautical left-hand down a bit here and there. True, one or two of the ladies' flowered hats were knocked wonky as we cannoned off the odd bridge pillar, but other than that all was tranquil.

For the time being.

Our picnic site was a murmurous meadow, shimmering in the heat, peopled by poppies and fluttering butterflies. Cows stood hock-high in watery reed beds, goggling at the goings on. The countryside languished and preened, pigeons burbled, doves cooed. At lunch we juggled hard-boiled eggs, jugs of juice, and received cordial advice of the 'Don't eat that wasp' variety. The day wore on. The afternoon river flowed, slowed, stopped, stretched and imperceptibly set off back the way it had come. Dudley and I didn't notice. We'd both died of boredom hours ago.

The guide books will tell you 'the River Arun is a major Sussex watercourse … a charming waterway that becomes increasingly attractive beyond Arundel where a castle overlooks the river … '

What they don't tell you is the river has a glint in its eye. As we started to trickle homewards, the H_2O began to buck up.

The Arun is the second fastest flowing river in Britain. Not a problem, of course, on a day when the sun was in its heaven, the wind in our hair, the breeze on our cheek. Merrily we bowled along, cries of merriment filling the air.

'Mind that weeping willow, it'll flay us alive.'

You will recall our mooring was alongside another craft, out near the centre of the stream. This fact began to assume significance. I don't know what mph we were doing when we sighted the mooring. It was below Mach 1, but above that at which you would alight from an omnibus.

'There she is, won't be long before we're home.'

The plan was to come alongside, grab hold, tie up and disembark. The world grew quiet as we began our final approach. The world grew noisy again as we arrived. Ba-boom! Beam to beam, we cannoned off majestically. The sound put up every bird in the Arun valley. I've never seen so many herons. Hands that had reached for the ship were pulled loose by the momentum. All except one.

A nameless novitiate, in an act of selfless devotion, had grabbed a porthole and clung on first with one hand then, miraculously, with the other. With superhuman strength, he hung on to the mother ship! Unfortunately he didn't hang on to the daughter ship. Plucked, is the word. Clinging on to the proposed mooring he was, with the aid of old man river, plucked from his seat among us.

Dudley and Dudley's best friend looked on with a lively interest.

The novice was now hanging perpendicular to the porthole, straight as an hour hand at six o'clock, up to his trouser pockets in Arun. Then, as we watched in horror - mixed with a lively interest - under the tug of the tide he swung like a pendulum to somewhere around eight o'clock Greenwich mean time. The yells went up.

'Hold on! Turn around! Back! We're coming, hang on!'

We weren't coming, we were going. And fast. With immense effort, oars flashing and crashing, our boat was turned. We barely held our own against the flood. Stretching every sinew, we inched towards the marooned cleric. About this time, his stretched sinews could take no more. His arms, which had doubled in length, gave way and he fell in. His cassock ballooned up in a circle around his waist like a black rubber dinghy. By now, rowing flat out, we were still motionless in midstream. He wasn't. He was spinning gently, but gathering pace. Like a giant black water lily he sailed past, just out of reach, and headed off towards Midhurst. As he went by, one of our crew raised his hat politely and said:

'Good day, Father,'

'Keep your hat on and keep rowing,' bellowed the bosun.

The floater raised a long, limp arm and gave a tidal wave. One of Uncle Reg's favourite sayings was to invite someone to 'take a walk till your hat floats'. This came to mind, as I'd never seen it done before. The Arun, I'm pleased to say, was in playful mood that day. It gave up its prey a short distance upstream. The lily drifted ashore and camouflaged itself in the mud and slime on the bank. We berthed and sent a search party. Fifteen men stood on the dead man's chest before they found him floundering beneath them. They upended him and poured back the unwanted river water. After he'd been through the car wash he was the hero of the hour. And to think, the adults had laid on this entertainment all by themselves.

Dudley and I had to admit it. We were impressed.

Chapter XVI
'From the shelter of my mind.'

So it was we returned to London to the succour of the sirens. One new feature had sprung up at the Stamford Bridge end of Holmead Road, two actually. A pair of brick-built air raid shelters; pink brick with flat slabs of concrete on top like lids. One was outside Billy Skinner's house, opposite the stonemason's, the other by Mr. Brown's.

I can still see all the doorways along there.

From our front door, number 477, you went past the top saloon door. Next was the entrance to the al fresco urinal. Then came the locked entrance to dustbin passage. Then the big double-gates of the builder's yard, proprietor Ernie French, neighbour, customer and family friend, who wore a Dodger Green trilby and had a pencil moustache. Next to this was a single door, the pedestrian entrance to Frenchy's yard. Move on again. Now a shop with boarded and shuttered windows. Next came another set of double-doors, glazed at the top, part of the first house in the Holmead Road terrace. This was the stonemason's, its tiny front garden full of blocks of stone and marble. People were still carving out a living, despite the hostile environment for the arts.

The new shelters proved of great interest, especially to those who may have been unaware of the nearby gents. The insides stank. This may be why the neighbourhood was reluctant to take refuge in them during air raids. I can't be sure. But I can be sure of the exact distance between the two shelters. This length became enshrined in local legend because of the way it was measured.

It was known as a Riddell.

One of the flowers of our forest was a certain Charlie Riddell, a genial soul. One day the assembled were gathered between the two shelters - the spot had rapidly become the in place - and Charlie graced us with his presence. He was standing, leaning really, up against one wall examining a flattened tanner someone was trying to pass on to him as a legal shilling. Nobody's fool, he was studying the currency minutely, turning it over and over between his fingers. Then he dropped it. Instantly he bent down, folding fluently from the waist, in the easy way you do when you're eight years old.

From then on it was a matter of simple mechanics.

As his head went down, his bum stuck out. It's not rocket science. Well, it is if you're standing too close to a wall at the time. He rocketed across the gap, bent at right angles, heading for the facing wall. In a few off balance strides he reached it and flung his forehead into the brickwork. You can imagine the result. Joy. The purest ecstasy. What a star! Charlie's chums fell rejoicing to the tarmac. They knew the first rule of first aid: hold your sides to prevent them splitting. It was some time before they got Charlie upright and led him home, still leaking. So it was the Riddell was born. We had the measure of our times.

Which is more than can be said for poor Mr. Brown.

Mr. Brown was a neighbour and he was not having a good war. I'm ashamed to say we tormented him to distraction. He lived opposite the front door of 477 at the top of the end house of Moore Park Road. On the Holmead Road side was a huge, flat windowless wall, brick from the ground to the first storey, then clad to the roof with wooden planking. It was a poster site, but there were no posters back then. At pavement level, a single door led inside to a rickety old staircase that zigzagged up to the top floor flat where Mr. Brown lived out his days. He was a 'most peculiar man'.

He was old in ways that are no longer fashionable, hermit old. He looked like the Irish playwright, George Bernard Shaw, but I suppose even GBS's once famous image is now forgotten. Brownie, as we called him, was frail, thin and bald. He had a straggly tobacco-stained, once-white beard and an unexpected turn of speed if he came after you waving his walking stick.

97

What boy could resist such a challenge?

The target was not him of course. It was the wooden wall. The wall was so big that even a wildly kicked or thrown ball would find the mark and bounce back to the sportsman below. It was perfect for catching practice. With every throw, every kick, the ball would bang on the wood, and the wood would amplify the sound between plank and wall and Mr. Brown would be driven further into his dementia. There was no window he could open to drive us off. The only way he could get to us was to come down several floors, open the door and deliver his message before climbing his weary way back up.

This he did.

He asked. He cajoled. He pleaded. We'd cease for a day or two, and then go back to torturing. Eventually he gave up being nice. We wrecked him. Not deliberately, just uncaringly. We reduced him to mania. We'd hear nothing from him for a while as a new tension brewed. Then, suddenly, clattering down the rickety staircase would come the rickety mad old man, bursting through the doorway, clearing the steps like a broken gazelle, maniacally brandishing his white walking stick. God! Was he blind as well? No, he can't have been, that stick got too close for Braille. Mr. Brown must have looked on us in the same way we look on terrorists, a torment and threat that won't go away until they grow up.

Was Billy Skinner with us on the infamous occasion at the other bomb shelter, the one in King's Road? I don't know. Our gang was a loose coalition convened from whoever was about on the day.

Billy basked in a reflected glow of fame twice removed. His older brother worked as secretary to none other than Lady Docker. Lady Docker was not a job description. She, Norah, was wife to Sir Bernard Docker, Chairman of Daimler, which was owned by the BSA Company. They were A-list celebs, the Posh and Becks of the day. They had a Daimler saloon car upholstered with real zebra skin and a matching gold-plated 860-ton yacht, the Shemara. Not in Holmead Road of course, but we'd seen it in the newspapers so it must be true.

BSA, the Birmingham Small Arms Company, made everything from bullets to bikes. During the Boer War they supplied rifles to the British. I wonder if Grandpa Millard had one? In the First World War their factories were turned over almost entirely to munitions. Mum may have worked in one of them. BSA was on the case again in World War 2. They produced nearly half a million of the Browning machine guns with which RAF Spitfires and Hurricanes won the Battle of Britain; one and a quarter million service rifles; 400,000 Sten guns; machine guns, cannon, antitank rifles and gun carriages, ten million shell fuses, over three and a half million magazines and 750,000 anti-aircraft rockets. And they were still called a Small Arms Company!

Birmingham must be a mighty tough town.

The Dockers were in the papers more than fish and chips. And we knew the younger brother of someone, who not only knew them, but worked for them! Could life get more exciting? Yes, it could, and it was about to do so.

The bomb shelter in King's Road was underground, unlike those in Holmead Road. It was built on a bombed site, one the Germans had made earlier. It was just by Tetcott Road. There was a bus stop there too. We went there to play because there were two ramps above the entrance stairs. We could climb these and slide down. We rarely went down into the shelter because of the smell.

The 45° angle ramps were purpose built for running up, and seeing how long you could hang on to the top edge before your grip gave way, and you slithered back down. This pursuit could occupy the finest minds all day long.

We weren't fashion victims back then. In fact, dress code played little part in our activities but on this occasion it came into focus. One of our number, I can't recall who, was lying at the top of the slope hanging by his fingertips. In fact, he was going for a record hang-on. We were doing our best to assist by throwing stones at him, flicking elastic bands at his bare legs, the usual team spirit. He was laughing. We were laughing.

He was yelling that he couldn't hang on. Yes you can we encouraged, still stoning him. His laugh grew more manic. That was when the dress code came to mind. Like the rest of us, he was wearing short trousers. From the tube of the right trouser leg there appeared a trickle - at first - of moisture. It darkened the black tarmac of the slide. He was doing what passers-by usually did down inside the shelter. This was no joke. This was hysterical. Our screams of mirth drew the attention of the queue at the nearby bus stop. They were appreciative. These were grim times and it doesn't take much to divert someone waiting for a Number 11 bus. The cling-on kid was howling with delight. The stream became a torrent and kept coming, the piddle puddling at the foot of the slope. We knew, he knew, the bus stop queue knew, that when his grip failed he would slide down his own damp patch and land in his own resevoir. The queue prayed their Number 11 bus wouldn't arrive before the climax of the show. It didn't. They saw it all in full. It was the last thing they would see for a while. That's when the bomb went off.

For some reason at that moment, I had gone part way down the shelter stairs. Suddenly there was a shout, then a tremendous roaring noise, more shouts and shrieks:

'Doodlebug! Buzz bomb!'

Despite racing up the stairs, out of the shelter, everyone saw it but me. The V1 flying bomb, the first modern guided missile, passed low overhead, travelling east to west, towards the Nell Gwynne pub. Myth had it if you could hear a V1, you were safe. The danger time was when the engine cut and the missile, with its 1870lb warhead, silently went into its terminal dive. It was no myth.

There was a silence.

Then came a concussing detonation, so immense, so viscerally shattering, as if the laws of physics themselves had been violated. There was no blinding flash, instead an instant blinding darkness. Dust erupted from the ground in a vast impenetrable brown cloud. The sky, the world disappeared in a choking, spitting, coughing miasma of terror, a gross defilement beyond defining.

'It's the Nell Gwynne! The Nell Gwynne!'

Run! Run! We ran, we couldn't run. You couldn't see to run. Through the grit-filled air came the retching thought - maybe not the Nell Gwynne! Maybe! No! No! Not the Sun! No! People were scattering blindly each in their own distraction. We reached the bridge over the railway. The Nell Gwynne was intact. Race on. Holmead Road was slightly clearer. The fog of war was beginning to descend, the dark brown turning yellow as the grit and debris fell from the air. Home was safe and the son was hugged tearfully to it. Inside, the whole house, the bedrooms, the bars, even the cellar were full of the enveloping dust cloud.

The bomb had landed over a quarter of a mile away, by the gasworks near Bagley's Lane. We heard of one survivor found nearby on a second floor, still sitting at a piano, the walls around them gone, their world torn open beyond comprehension.

Chapter XVII
'I'm here.'

'Rose!'

'I'm here!'

'Ro-o-se!'

'I'm coming. I'm here!'

'Rose, fetch me this, please.'

'It's coming. I'm coming. I'm here!'

'Rose, fetch me that, please.'

'It's on its way. I've got it. I'm coming. I'm here!'

Rose Hainsby 'did' for us. She was our daily. She was Rose the pinafore, Rose the yellow duster, Rose the Brasso, Rose the midmorning glass of Reid's stout, taken in the kitchen sitting in front of the ice box, or it may have become a fridge by then.

'Where are you Rose?'

'I'm here.'

'Please, Rose.'

'I'm coming. I'm here!'

She was five foot nothing or smaller, ageless beyond years and much damaged by war. Sadly, she would be even more damaged by the peace. Rose was growing down as I was growing up. I could almost see her shrinking. She didn't have many teeth but those still in residence were pegged in the smile of the eternally put upon. Her kind face, often washed with tears, had a kind of gratitude that someone, anyone - even me - was still bothering to put upon her. She walked - hobbled almost - with a rolling, shoulder-swaying gait that pained her every pace. You winced just to watch her. She walked the walk and talked the talk of war. There was a Fulham footballer of the time, Ronnie Rook, famous for his bandy legs. He had nothing on Rose. She was parenthetical.

'Ooh, my poor feet,' she'd say. 'I'm here.'

Rose was a mainstay of the team who made up my support group. She cleaned up after me, picked up after me, made beds after me, and often - enraged at my antics - she would have willingly chased after me if Hitler hadn't broken her legs in God knows how many places.

Did he also kill her husband at the same time? I'm not sure.

Rose had been 'bombed out' as it was called.

I don't know where she was 'bombed out' from. It may have been from the shelter site in King's Road, the one with the two slopes. There was another possibility, a little further along

King's Road towards World's End. In fact, I think this was the more likely spot. There was a block of flats that stood there, the Guinness Trust Buildings. They were hit, I'm fairly sure of that. Anyway, from whatever rubble Rose was pulled, she was now living in requisitioned housing in Maxwell Road, a few of streets away from The Rising Sun.

The pub, in easy walking distance even for her, became her home from home. When she wasn't working, which wasn't often, Rose could usually be found in the private bar. This was the fourth of the Sun's quartet of hospitality suites. It was a tiny snug of a bar where the less extrovert took their ease. It was a place of slippered feet, hairnets and curlers, of bottled stout and Guinness; of headscarves and Mrs. Potts from number three. A place of authenticity beyond any TV soap's imaginings.

There were two facing wooden benches with big wooden wings, like clubmen's chairs. These could take three diminished souls side by side. When Rose was ensconced you could barely see her over the top of the counter. It was only the occasional: 'I'm here!' that alerted you to her presence. There were two other benches, doubles these, either side of the door that opened to Holmead Road.

The private bar was also our off-licence, our export market.

Out went the pints and quarts, the bottles that kept up the spirits of the needy during closing hours; out went the packets of cigarettes in 10s and 20s, Gold Flake, Player's and Woodbines; out too went the Smith's Crisps, with their twist of blue paper full of salt to keep your blood pressure perky. The private bar was the industrial heart of our takeaway and saw a lot of traffic. But it wasn't mainstream. It was a branch line compared to the mainline express of the business.

The engine of the whole enterprise was, of course, Stamford Bridge.

And through the football crowds, the crush, the chaos, Rose would always be there. Many's the time on a mad Saturday, the place heaving with the parched, a tiny hand, knobbed with arthritis, would squeeze up between the massed ranks of the throng, holding an empty half-pint glass. No matter how rushed you were, if you were serving, you popped another bottle of Reid's into the frail fingers. Glass, hand and bottle would withdraw into the jostling mass of bodies with only a distant 'I'm here' amid the clamour to acknowledge receipt.

Mad Saturdays, Chelsea home game Saturdays that is, were truly mad, mad beyond imagining. For years I was too small to help out behind the bar. For years I was too idle to help. And then, for what seemed like years, I helped. In later years I played squash, an active game. But never on a squash court did I sweat more than on a home game Saturday in the Sun. There might be as many as ten of us serving. You couldn't have more staff because we'd get in each other's way and there were only four tills.

'Three pints of stout and mild, a half of bitter, three light ales, two gin and tonics, a Muscado, two ham sandwiches and three packets of crisps, please.'

'£3 2s 6d! thank you!'

Remembering the cost of everything and doing the mental arithmetic so fast the customers couldn't believe it, was something you did, not something you enjoyed. Forgetting the cost of anything on sale was one of the things guaranteed to drive Reg up the wall.

'Uncle Reg, how much is a port and lemon?'

His eyeballs would be swivelling like a one armed bandit's under the strain of his own computations.

'1/6d,' he'd mutter with a glare.

Upstairs Mum would be Chief of the Imperial General Staff in the kitchen, marshalling the troops, making more sandwiches. She was the finest sandwich maker in a powerful team. She could slice ham so thin it was like tracing paper.

'The secret,' she'd say, 'is to let lots of meat hang over the edge of the bread. That way customers think the sandwich is stuffed full!'

The dumb waiter, now repaired, would whirl up and down. Heaped plates full of sandwiches, sausage rolls and Scotch eggs would be sent down to feed the five thousand. The very building throbbed and jumped with manic activity. The place would get so packed people couldn't get in or out. It was mayhem. Then, as kick-off time approached the crush would thin. That's when collecting the empties would begin, hundreds, maybe thousands of glasses to be hand-washed, dried and polished ready for the rush after the game and following that, the 'dogs' in the evening.

Outside the ground, up to their ankles in litter, paperboys offered their wares, The Star, Evening News and Evening Standard. These became:

'Star, Nooz 'n' Stan'ard! Orla winners 'n' 'arf times, read orl abaht it! Star, Nooz 'n' Stan'ard!

The 'dogs' was the evening Greyhound Racing meeting after the football. This rush was nothing like the throng at lunchtime, but it was big enough. Come mid-evening, nine o'clock-ish, the dog crowd would drift away and the pub would begin to fill with locals. Counter-Crusher with her gin-and-it, took up her place of residence for the evening, for the duration, for the long years of her tenure during which no one moved her or her bar stool so much as one inch from her place in the main saloon. There'd always be someone at the piano - sometimes it was Uncle Jack - and the singing would begin.

'There'll be bluebirds over the white cliffs of Dover ... '

Time gentlemen, please, time ladies and gentlemen, please, let's be 'aving you, come along there, please.

'Hurry up please it's time.'

Outside, the singing would go on for a while, then fade to talking as those reluctant to go home stood in the lamp light around the blue police phone box.

'Goonight Bill. Goonight Lou. Goonight May. Goonight. Ta ta. Goonight. Goonight.'

Rose grew older. I grew taller. She was unhappy. I didn't know why.

Around this time, with me now in long trousers, there was an event, an exhibition, near Fulham Town Hall, perhaps organised by the Town Hall. I don't know what political party was the driving force. The idea was architectural. Two of the terraced houses in Cedarne Road had been knocked together into one. I can't recall the details. It may be that they had been converted into one big dwelling. Perhaps the two top floors were made into one flat and likewise the two ground floors. No matter. The result to my mind was brilliant. This was the future. In a world of utility signs, to see such a makeover fifty years before the word was coined was eye opening. To see space created other than by high explosives was a pleasure. The modern furniture, the lighting, the comfort, the luxury after the long years of everything being rationed, including ideas, was inspiring. Every terraced house I'd been in up till then was filled with nothing but the smell of boiled cabbages.

This was a time of building and rebuilding. Opportunity had knocked. Hitler had knocked down half of the country's building stock. What better moment to restore, replenish, rehouse? High-fives were given to high-rise towers. Manhattan was coming to Blighty. And it was happening now.

One by one, Rose's neighbours and friends in Maxwell Road, were moved away to their new high-rise homes. Good-bye Bill. Good-bye Lou. Good-bye May. Good-bye. Ta ta. Good-bye. Good-bye. The requisitioned property Rose lived in was neglected.

The plumbing and the heating didn't work properly. The roof leaked. Assurances were given. Reassurances were given.

'Won't be long now, Luv, we'll have you out of here. Just you hang on.'

The two-edged sword hovered. The prospect of a new home appealed. The prospect of the loss of everything else appalled. The council continued the destruction of the neighbourhood, started by the Wehrmacht. They saw the future through rose coloured glasses. It wasn't Rose's vision. She knew the move would mean the loss of her beloved Sun.

One day I went to Maxwell Road to see the hovel that was her home.

Look back in anger, someone wrote. It is easy to see why. Rose was the only person left living in the dilapidated building. The house was derelict, cold and damp. A bare bulb hung from a flex in the centre of the stained ceiling. The grimy window at the back overlooked the overgrown garden.

'Can you see them, Jimmy? Can you? There, look there!'

I could see them. Rats, running, scurrying, hurrying; two, three, six, ten or more, racing through the wilderness.

Gentrification of the area was decades away. When it came, it was rumoured Diana Dors, a film star of the time, bought a house in Maxwell Road. I wonder which one?

Then came the time to move. Rose said good-bye to the rats and moved up in the world, eight floors up. She was rehoused in the jewel-in-the-crown of high-rise blocks, the Clem Attlee estate on Lillie Road. Was it Hugh Dalton House? Those good men, eminent politicians full of goodwill, did little good for Rose.

As the crow flies, Hugh Dalton House was three-quarters of a mile from the Sun. For Rose, it could have been in Australia. The private bar and the mid-morning Reid's stout were a cripplingly long way off. Rose's lifeline, I believe, were her nephews and nieces I think - of whom she often spoke.

To my shame I visited her only once.

The tower block was as expected. The residents had pissed in the lifts and signed their artwork by scratching their names on the walls. This wasn't a problem. The lifts didn't work anyway. And what were eight flights of stairs to me?

Rose greeted me with thanks-for-coming tears. She waited on me with cups of tea as she'd done a million times before.

There was nothing to say. She'd kept her bare bulb. The desolation was abject minus the rats.

Time passed. Outside her window, the magnificent cloudscape of west London beckoned.

'Good-bye, good-bye,' she said, and clung to me, her tearful face barely up to my chest. 'Good-bye, thanks for coming, Jimmy, you always was a good boy.'

She cried and wept. We both knew we'd never meet again. 'I'm here,' would become I'm not here. With the awkwardness of youth, I bent and kissed the top of her head. Beyond the window, the westering sun sank into the fire of its own diffusion.

'And the fire and the Rose are one.'

Chapter XVIII
Cold play.

Was it world's first mass truancy? It would have been if the headmaster, Mr Guy Boas, hadn't given the school the afternoon off to see the football, Moscow Dynamos versus Chelsea at Stamford Bridge.

Entrance money! Who needs entrance money? Forget the turnstiles, follow me. The scholars flooded along Fulham Road, turned right into Billing Road, left into Billing Place, over the railings at the end, down the embankment, cross the railway lines, clamber up the chain-link fence, then spider down the other side.

You were in, the holy of holies, Stamford Bridge.

Pepper was in. Bishop was in. Croft was in. Harrison was in. 'Where's Bushsell? Anyone seen Pickerton?'

Many were caught and thrown out. Many more melted into the crowd. It wasn't hard to lose yourself among 85,000 people dressed in demob grey. It was iron cold, a November day of shivering mists and palpitating excitement, men and boys trailing empty speech bubbles of their own breath. Illegal entry had never been in such a good cause. There were 85,000 in a space for 40,000, with 15,000 locked out and trying to break in. The police were barely able to get a good view for themselves. The great break in rivalled the great escape from Stalag Luft III. The crush was enormous. I hadn't felt anything like it since VJ - Victory over Japan - night on Westminster Bridge.

That was when, around midnight, because of the crush and panic Dudley and I were manhandled over the top of the mob for the full length of the Mother of Parliaments. We were put in separate ambulances and ferried home along with other flattened celebrants, some of them sober.

And in the football crush, where did your correspondent view the match of the century up to that time? Thanks to Uncle Reg, from the comfort of the Chelsea director's box.

Russia at Stamford Bridge! The bridge between two worlds, with the world's war weary eyes focused on this most massive of games. The Dynamo Moscow club was backed by the NKVD, the Soviet secret police. They were the personal favourites of the dreaded Lavrenty Beria who headed the hated police. They had won four of the first seven Russian league titles. The pressure on them to win was huge. They weren't on a goodwill tour of Britain. They were on a good-win tour or nothing, nothing but Siberia.

'He's-not-your-real-father-you-know' may not have been my real father but I clung to him like he was on this and a thousand other sporting occasions. Time after time, Uncle Reg managed to produce the magic tickets. Admittedly there was no seat available for me in the director's box. What of that! The privilege, the thrill, just to be there, sitting on the steps.

'Uncle Reg, Uncle Reg, I'm sitting on the steps! Steppes! Geddit?

He got it. He was probably thinking to himself: 'He's not my real son, you know.'

From the steps I watched the overspill of the crowd as they were allowed on to the pitch to sit by the touchline. Every eye was on the Chelsea captain and right back, John Harris, who wore his shirtsleeves rolled down in an early fashion statement.

John Harris, the referee, and the Dynamo Moscow captain, Mikhail Semichastny, went through an overlong ritual of tossing the coin. It took ages. With hindsight this small act of theatre presaged many of the misunderstandings of the cold war that came along soon after.

In Russia, the way they choose ends is simple. The referee offers two pieces of paper to the captains; one reads 'kick-off', the other 'choice of ends'. The British coin-tossing routine, which could have been explained in the dressing rooms, was laboriously spelled out in full view of the 85,000. The delay added to the impression, already being whipped up by the press, of the Johnny-foreigner-ness of these Johnny-foreigners. As for Dynamo's pre-match courtesy of presenting each member of the Chelsea team with a posy of flowers, well, the look on centre-forward Tommy Lawton's face spoke volumes, even to those sitting on the distant steps.

At school, of course, it didn't do to boast about being in the director's box. That was something to be kept to yourself. And - keep this to yourself - I didn't take the Billing Place route into the ground. I told everyone I did, because that's what the others had done, but I didn't need to.

I went in through the front gates, clinging to Uncle Reg's coat tails.

Week after week, I was either in the director's box at Stamford Bridge to see Chelsea, or the equal box at Craven Cottage to see Fulham, where Reg's brother, Frank Osborne, was manager. I walked across the road to one venue and was chauffeured to the other in Uncle Reg's green Standard Eight, EGP 626; and later in his bigger Standard saloon, and finally in the walnut and leather world of his cherished Rover 90.

I missed nothing, internationals, cup-ties, the lot.

Who was at Wembley when Wilf Mannion, covered in blood, was heroically stretchered off with fractured a cheekbone against the Scots? Whose face can be seen in the crowd the day Stanley Matthews won his cup winner's medal? Who was in the best seats when Nat Lofthouse was the two-goal hero of Bolton's FA Cup Final triumph over Manchester United? Who saw Ferenc Puskas and the Hungarians drub England? We went to all the big cup-ties, the semis at Villa Park, 'the best dressing rooms in the league,' Reg would say. We went to almost every cup final, every England home game for a decade or more.

I didn't know I was born. And it wasn't only football.

We saw Len Hutton creaming cover drives at the Oval. We saw Denis Compton brylcreeming boundaries at Lords. Rhamadin and Valentine bowling their calypsos. Jim Laker of Surrey bowling all before him. Miller and Lindwall with the world and its ashes at their feet. Bobby Locke imperious at Wentworth. Ice hockey, with Chick Zamick, the Nottingham Panther. Speedway with Tommy Price, the Wembley Lion.

The Wembley what?

Wembley Lions were one of speedway's top teams. Motorcycle dirt track racing was huge back then. It kept the wolf from the doors of Wembley Stadium after the war. If it weren't for speedway, the FA wouldn't have had a Wembley Stadium. And without Wembley, there would have been no 1948 Olympic Games for Britain. It's possible there may not have been an England World Cup soccer triumph in 1966.

Week after week the Wembley speedway crowds were vast: 65,000 versus New Cross, 23 May;

76,000 versus Belle Vue, 20 June;

67,000 versus New Cross, 4 July;

85,000 versus West Ham, 11 July.

At the final Wembley meeting, on October 3, over 100,000 supporters arrived. The gates were closed with 20,000 fans outside listening on loudspeakers. The crowd was so big half the Fleet Street reporters couldn't get in until the interval. That was the mad night when the Wembley skipper rode a rocket-assisted bike! Speedway aces such as Tommy Price, Bill Kitchen and Split Waterman, were stars. The Wembley Speedway Supporters Club was the biggest in the world, with 65,000 members - ten times bigger than Manchester United at that time. Just imagine what the sport might have been if there had been TV in those days.

Even more magically, Reg took Dodger Green, Janaway and me to see Cassius Clay, as he was then, beat Henry Cooper. Clay swaggered into the cauldron of the Empire Pool, robed and towelled and wearing a golden crown on his head! We saw 'the blond bomber' Billy Walker versus Johnny Prescott in a gladiatorial bout that everyone agreed couldn't be bettered. Then, when they met in the rematch, it was even better.

I didn't only see stars I met them. They'd come into the Sun. It was normal for Chelsea players to pop in for a quick half before a game. They certainly came in after the match. It's a thirsty business, ninety minutes of first division football.

That's how this hand that holds the mouse shook the hand of the great Tommy Lawton himself.

These were different times. The game was slower, the players less fit, the pitches were swamps or frozen solid. The globe hadn't warmed, the winters were colder. The players wore boots that might have been chiselled from the living rock. There were none of 'your fancy running pumps' of today. The footballs were like cannon balls. A header could ram your skull into your ribcage.

The names would echo down the years: Stanley Matthews, Tom Finney, Tommy Lawton, Raich Carter, Wilf Mannion. So do the results: England 10, Portugal 0 in Lisbon; England 4, Italy 0 in Turin. We listened to these away internationals crouched over our radio. They were the only matches for which Reg couldn't get tickets. Whatever the result, if Matthews had played you knew some left back was spending the evening at his osteopath having his legs unknotted.

Soccer stars weren't the only regulars in the Sun. Wherever sports stars can be seen, so can journalists. One quartet of writers was especially welcome. They worked for a long gone paper, The Sunday Pictorial and wrote a column bylined, The Four Just Men. It was forthright, opinionated, balanced, and reliable, blazing with integrity. How could it not be? The combined experience of four experts gave you the benefit of their first hand, on-the-spot wisdom.

That reminds me, we haven't yet had a tour of the big room in the Rising Sun.

The big room - our 'best' sitting room - was off to the left of the tiny passage that led to the little room and it may have contributed to the myth of Old Man Kelso's fortune. In the same way the bars downstairs were furnished with many pictures - original artworks by the sports cartoonist, Tom Webster, and lots of photographs of Old Man Kelso at his golf - so the big room was expensively furnished and boasted several fine Victorian oil paintings. These were mainly Scottish landscapes, cattle up to their hocks in reed beds at sunset, that sort of thing. A three-seater Chesterfield, covered in rust-brown velvet, graced the left wall. Handsome wing back chairs stood either side of the gas fire to the right. On the floor was a costly Persian carpet from Harrods. The upright piano was behind the door. Centre stage was a shining dining table kept lovingly polished by 'I'm here'. The table could be extended to take eight diners on special occasions. On match Saturdays, the extension leaves were down and four chairs were put in place, one each for the Four Just Men.

That's where they played cards and kept a bottle or two of Scotch and a soda siphon company during those long Saturday afternoons when Chelsea were at home to some dull opponent. Uncle Reg - and his sidekick - would go to the match and bring home the news at the end of the game. The writers often knew the result before we got back. The windows of the room faced Stamford Bridge and they could guess at the score by the number and volume of cheers. Armed with Reg's detailed news, the match report would be written and phoned through on Fulham 4654. Outside the windows, the retail arm of the news trade advertised their wares directly to the target audience.

'Star, Nooz 'n' Stan'ard! Orla winners 'n' 'arf times, read orl abaht it! Star, Nooz 'n' Stan'ard!'

Chapter XIX
A thorny problem.

'He made you.'

'He made me what?'

'No, no. He made you. He created you.'

A pause.

'Oh.'

This was rather like the question after my trip in the dumb waiter. I didn't think of a better reply until much later. Who was talking to me? Pretty well everyone, certainly all those grown ups who were interested in my spiritual development, as they put it. The 'He' in question was, of course, 'He' of the thorny hat. Actually, I was led to believe it wasn't Him who made me, but his dad. Confused? Me too. There was also a ghost in the story somewhere. I was too young to know the word sceptical, but not too young to experience the feeling. From the moment I saw those pictures in the convent at Wealdstone, I knew I didn't like this story. The images put me off. If today, you knew someone who downloaded that sort of thing from the web, you'd be suspicious. I may have been young, but I'd already developed a desire to keep my heart inside my chest wall. That's the place for hearts, not floating about on their own, glowing and leaking blood.

But Mum wanted me to believe, so I said did.

Our local church was the Servite in Fulham Road. It had a font in the entrance, like a birdbath, full of 'holy' water. I learned to make the sign of the cross - Reg called it doing the ace-king-queen-jack. I learned to genuflect like I used to back in my Marist Convent days. I did all this willingly. My '...in nomine patrie...' was the fastest in west London. Not that I had much competition. None of my friends went to church. That was one reason I didn't like it. Mum and Marg usually took me, but they were family, they didn't count. There was no one to play with. Uncle Reg never went, although I'm sure he could have got tickets if he'd wanted to.

'He's a proddy-waddy', Mum would say, her term for a protestant.

The congregations were large. Not as large as at Wembley for the speedway, but big. They were mainly made up of women, about 70%-30%, with a few children and a fair number of babies. Worshipping was dull, hour after hour of wishing you were somewhere else. It was like going to school in your own time. I didn't understand a word. The mass was in Latin. Oddly, this was a good thing; at least it preserved some sense of mystery. Later mass was said in English and understanding merely contributed to my incredulity. The food - communion wafers - was awful, little roundels of nameless mouth-drying stuff, not in the same league as Mum's roundels of hard-boiled egg. Even if I'd liked them, there were never enough to go round. You were given only one and that made you gag. I was scared to look at the pictures on the walls 'the stations of the cross' as they were called. They were stations at which I didn't want to get off. They scared me more than Jimmy Bledlow and the khaki torch. There was a curious mismatch too.

These Sunday morning masses were peaceful, respectful and solemn. The church was always nearly full. They weren't like the rowdy crowds at Stamford Bridge. Yet the spiritual folk surrounded themselves with images of extreme violence. There were life-size statues of mutilated bodies, bloodied and butchered. It seemed to me that if anybody would have use for this sort of imagery, it would be the 85,000 baying for blood at the Bridge. But no.

The raucous football crowds had amiable mascots like Stamford The Lion, while the devout were singing solemn hymns while gazing at scenes of scourging and mutilation. There was a lesson here, but I'm not sure it was the one I was supposed to learn.

Come to think of it, we had several figurines at home. These were of a hooded and robed lady, not a nun. She was wearing blue and white and held in one hand an amputated heart. Her other hand was held aloft with two fingers raised, like an umpire giving some luckless soul out lbw.

One thing I did like about church was the music. Not the hymn singing, that was vile, though I mimed along in order to show willing. I'd mouth the words with head held high, tonsils gaping, never uttering a sound. No, the music I liked, was the proper singing by the choir with the organ. At high mass, as opposed to low mass - don't ask - the cast would tog up in their best robes, light the incense bucket - the smoke had the kick of a chlorine tablet - and on would come choir and organ. I loved that. It taught me to love a good choir and loathe organs - a wanton waste of wind - although I've since met many a charming organist. But even to my disaffected ears some of the church music was affecting.

The reading matter though, well, that was another matter. It was duller than the hymns. One of the books I came across was the Book of Common Prayer. This was well thought of at home, which surprised me. Mum usually didn't like anything common. The edges of the pages were covered in gold leaf and, to my mind that was the only thing about them that sparkled. This, of course, was unfair. The book stood no chance. My library at this stage consisted of The Wizard, The Hotspur,

Beano and Dandy. All tales of adventure not containing Rockfist Rogan, Wilson the Wonderman, or Desperate Dan received scant attention.

So it was in the Servite Church, Fulham Road, my brain was washed, rinsed and hung out to dry in the post-war smog. It was all done in my best interests you understand, with great love, with the very best will in the world and all that. But brains are like socks; too much washing and they shrink. Of course, I swallowed all the instruction I was given. I questioned nothing. Perhaps, after all, 'He' did make me. Perhaps 'He' was my real father. Regrettably, Philip Wade Kelso had by now vanished from my memory. And if 'He' was who they said 'He' was, I wondered what tickets 'He' could get?

Chapter XX
The phantom inheritance.

Some years later I attended a Sunday lunch party, at a house decorated mostly in oatmeal, in London W2. Holding court on a sofa was a confident, articulate gent, a stranger of about my age who'd gathered about him a small audience of lovelies. His talk touched on, in part, his schooldays. He spoke, without boasting, but with affection, almost a touch of pride about his alma mater. How good that must feel, I thought, to be able to look back on one's education without your toes curling with embarrassment.

Then he named his school: Sloane School.

You remember the surprise when that bomb blew in the window in Kinsbourne Green? The effect was the same. There couldn't be two Sloane Grammar Schools, Hortensia Road, Chelsea, could there? The real surprise was that he was speaking with approval of the house of correction in which we had both done time. I'd never spoken about school since it and I had parted company.

Indeed, it was partly the parting company aspect that kept me quiet.

When I finally left the Marist Convent, I was sent straight to Sloane. Mum was tickled pink about this because she thought grammar schools housed a better class of layabout. And because Mum was pleased, I was pleased. Sloane had two things in its favour; it was only a short walk from home; and it was a Nazgul-free zone. But one thing I did not like. From day one I felt left out.

This was because I was left out.

I arrived for assembly on that first morning, punctual, scrubbed and eager for instruction, only to be told I couldn't join the assembly. Instead, I was put in a separate classroom with half-a-dozen other asylum seekers. We were disassembled. From the outset, I parted company with the majority, a lesion never to heal. And why? Because I was a catholic. The majority were protestants, Church of England. This gave me an odd feeling. Was I now two things: me, and a catholic? Of course, what had happened was I, like countless others before me had received, unasked for and unwanted, the world's most common gift.

The phantom inheritance.

It is assumed, without question, that offspring share their parent's beliefs. Mum was a catholic therefore I was. Fair enough in my case because, at that time, it was true. But it's

129

an unreasonable assumption if you think about it. Irrational beliefs, the most divisive and damaging weapon known to mankind, are passed on like hand-me-down clothes. I didn't know the child of a catholic is catholic only if he or she decides to be one. There's no biology involved, only belief. You inherit religion only if you want to. This is true of all beliefs. Choice is involved. As a child your freedom of choice is compromised because your family imprint you when you're at your most gullible. What do the Jesuits say: give us a child for the first few years and we've got them for life?

This was the first lesson, maybe the only lesson, I learned at school. So I became an outsider. It didn't bother me, it just was. Outside, beyond the classroom door where the outcasts sat, we could hear the assembled in the school hall welcoming the day with Onward Christian Soldiers and other military messages. I didn't mind. I could have silently mouthed their songs if they had let me in.

We were ghetto'd in that classroom at the back of the assembly hall, the one in the corner with the framed print of a van Gogh landscape on the wall outside the door. I didn't care much for M. van Gogh either, with his dauby French ways, not a single cow up to its hocks in reed beds.

I tried to look on the bright side of exclusion. I believe in the freedom to worship. I also believe people should be free to not make me worship. That would suit me fine. So there I sat, on the outside looking in. I was not alone though.

The other outcasts were a ragtag of beliefs and non-beliefs, sunk in the certainty of whatever superstition had been forced into them. In an odd way, I was grateful to them. Up till then, I had no idea there were other gods, let alone hundreds of them, all sorts, all over the world. Naturally, mine was the only true one, mine was best. I knew that. Finding out there were loads of gods made me realise, in a manner of speaking, we're all atheists. Whatever god you worship means you're not worshipping one of the others. In that sense you're an atheist. These thoughts didn't come in a rush, you understand, not on that first day. They dribbled in, you might say. Nobody spelled out the real deal to me. I wish they had. I wish someone had sat me down and said:

Listen, Sonny, this is how it is.

Throughout history, peoples all over the world have made up creation myths.

Some of these beliefs, like ships, have figureheads, single gods. Some have many gods. Some have no gods. But all religions have one thing in common. They all believe, with no proof, in life after death. Also, for some reason, none of the figurehead gods left any written words. Witnesses jotted down the things they said and these jottings have become, in various forms, the word. People believe in gods because they have faith. Faith means a strong belief in something without evidence or proof. It's a cop out. People kill each other over their beliefs. People believe fervently. People are at their most dangerous when filled with fervour. Beware of fervour. Whether you are flayed alive by crusaders, or bus bombed by suiciders, fervour is at the heart of it. Fervour is the true F-word of our times. One last thing, Sonny. Don't think science is just another belief system. It isn't. It differs fundamentally because, crucially, it demands proofs. Here endeth the first lesson. Got that, Sonny?

Sonny would have been quite pleased to have 'got that'.

It wouldn't have been too much to ask, would it? I think it would have been very helpful to Sonny at that stage. It would have established ground zero. In fact, I think it should be the preamble to all religious instruction. I doubt if anything or anybody would have changed much as a result of that little chat. People would still be free to believe in whatever religion they want, their 'delusion of choice'. Probably I would have said, 'Oh,' and gone on thinking Mum was right anyway. In fact, I'm sure I would. I'm not a boat rocker, never was.

However, one good result did come of all this religiosity. My immersion course in the catholic creation myth introduced me to three important things.

Paintings, grim ones agreed, but paintings none the less. Music, some of it good. And literature. I now knew exactly where I stood in the matter of The Wizard, The Hotspur, Beano and Dandy versus the Book of Common Prayer.

In a word, art. Art is important to me because it is an acronym. A for authority; R for revelation; T for tradition. Art reminds me that authority, revelation and tradition are bad reasons to believe anything. Authority usually means being told something is true by someone important, Mum in my case. Revelation - ye olde life changing experience - is based on powerful feelings, usually transcendental, someone has had in which they claim a truth has been shown to them. These feelings are often intense, emotional, profound and invariably, hogwash. Tradition means something is believed because it has been believed for a long time, not because it's true.

We live in spoon-bending times. Human beings are 'significance-junkies'.

Religion is an ongoing business. For example, although I didn't know it, about the time I was being excluded from assembly in Hortensia Road, in far away Rome the Catholic Church was adopting a new belief. This was the acceptance of the assumption, the ascension of the Virgin Mary - she of the figurine giving out lbw - into heaven. It was around then the ascension belief became official policy. Prior to that, it wasn't part of the catholic canon. Now, my schooldays may seem ancient to you, but to me they don't seem that long ago. And if the Catholic Church was still tinkering with the fundamentals of the religion when I was a kid, the everlasting quality, the eternality of all these beliefs begins to look shaky to say the least.

Why did no one tell me - why did no one tell Mum - that the word 'virgin' in the Greek Septuagint translation of the Hebrew scriptures is a mistranslation? The Hebrew word 'almah' (translated 'virgin' in the passage in Isaiah in the Septuagint) is a generic term that refers to a girl or any young woman, married or unmarried, virgin or not? I would like to have known this.

Filling young minds with questionable information and telling them it is true, is a form of child abuse. It's not as bad as sexual or physical abuse, or neglect, but it is an abuse and it casts a long shadow. In fairness, throughout these rites - or wrongs - of passage, no one ever laid a hand on me, excluding a few whacks from the whirling rosaries. There were never any sexual shenanigans. Yet my catholic guilt persists. All this led me to believe you should question everything, especially anything stemming from authority, revelation and tradition. Seek evidence. Seek proof. But, as I was soon to find out, if you do you will forever be in the minority. What evolutionary advantage gullibility imparts, I'm not sure. All I know is there's a lot of it about.

Now, what was that noise?

It was the noise of those feet in ancient time, tramping from the assembly hall. The outcasts trooped after them, with them but apart. We marched into the future, hungry for truth and knowledge about everything, not just creation myths and virgin births. Although, oddly, it wasn't long after this I began to develop an unexpected interest in the virgin of the species.

Chapter XXI
The dinge.

In a way I'd always felt there'd be more to it - life I mean - than was currently coming my way. Perhaps not always, but certainly from the time of the revelation. Yes, I know it's prudent to question anything based on revelation. But, as I was pleased to discover, there can be more than one type.

Coming home from school early one afternoon, struggling up the stairs, lugging my satchel, still in short trousers, long socks around my ankles, I chanced to spy a passing aunt on the landing. The good lady was coming from the bathroom. As she swept by in a cloud of talc her dressing gown briefly gaped and her bare right breast momentarily appeared. We didn't use nano seconds back then, but I can confirm the sighting was of limited duration. However, it was long enough to see the mammary on display bore an extraordinarily long nipple.

It is worth pointing out these were the days when a 'glimpse of stocking was something shocking'. As a result of this stupefying sight, satchel, long socks and short trousers reeled backwards down the stairwell coming to rest on the half-landing halfway down.

It has always interested me why certain things stay in the mind and others don't.

Retention seems to have nothing to do with merit, importance or the time taken to hoist the memory aboard. This image was indelibly embedded in the juvenile soup in no time at all. There was, I hasten to add, nothing of the Gypsy Rose Lee about the event. The virtuous lady in question, fresh from the tub, would have been mortified to know what I'd seen. This was no flash. It was pure chance. None the less, the lid had momentarily come off the fleshpot. The bathed and robed relative swept away to her boudoir, leaving the child choking on talcum powder yet with a curiously renewed interest in what life might hold.

That wasn't the end of the affair.

It so happened my artistic endeavours at this time were taken up with scenes of warfare, including many depictions of enemy U-boats. The current masterpiece showed a squadron of these evil craft. From some reason, the size of one of the U-boats on the far horizon became equated with the length of the recently sighted nipple. No nipple, of course could really have been that big, I know that. But I also know the one seen was undeniably prodigious.

It set a standard and led inevitably to disillusionment.

Later, when engaged in the fumbling disrobements of adolescence, there always escaped from me at the moment of denouement, a 'tut' of disappointment. And despite a lifetime spent in ever more desperate attempts to lay hands on the repositories of the milk of human kindness, the unholy grail forever escaped my grasp. Nipples have remained obstinately nipple-sized ever since, whereas I had glimpsed nipple nirvana. So, a retrospective apology to all who received 'tuts', not that there have been that many, more's the pity. However, to those who were adversely affected, I assure you the 'tuts' were nothing personal.

But what damage had this done to my soul?

I heard the word soul used a lot in my early world yet I had no idea what it meant or what it was. Useful word for sailors and pilots, though.

'Good morning, helicopter Golf Oscar Delta here, four souls on board, request permission to land, over.'

Unequivocal, that. No doubt about how many ruffians are headed your way when you get that message. Other uses of the word seemed more equivocal. I was told your soul was given to you, not by your parents, but by God. I'm not sure if all gods dole out souls, but the one round our way did. The soul I learned is immortal. It goes into you at the outset and stays until you die, at which point it leaves and then teams up with you again in the non-proven afterlife.

Okay, thanks Mum, can I go out and play now?

It didn't occur to me to ask when exactly the soul was given to you. When was the outset? When you were born? I don't want to be picky, but at what point? When you were half in, half out? Or maybe it wasn't at birth? Maybe it was when you were conceived? Probably not then; too indelicate handing out souls at a time like that.

I wasn't encouraged to ask questions, so I took it all on the nod. And soon other things began to occupy my mind.

One day, out of the blue, my genes came over all selfish, excessively so I thought. I remember thinking, calm down lads, I've got the message. But no, they clamoured for attention. From then on, my sex education was largely a do-it-yourself affair. My chosen journals, course papers and study articles were bought from Mr. Davis the newsagent, duly making sure there was no one else in the shop at time of purchase. Oddly - is this a Freudian cover-up - I can't recall the names of the girlie magazines employed in my thirst for knowledge. I do recall a fellow scholar saying they were all the same, 'full of pictures of women covered in netting'. True, but I tried to not let this distract me.

When I think back on this period, which I rarely do for fear of bringing on one of my dismay attacks, my main recollection is of the roof. You remember I told you about the roof garden? Well, there was one item I left out.

The Sun had two roofs.

On the wall to the left of the kitchen door, were drainpipes. You could shin up these, hop over the low parapet and on to the roof proper. No adult could reach me there. In this eyrie I beavered away at my studies.

My reveries were augmented by doodling anatomical fantasies. The drawings had a certain primitive cave-painting explicitness that would have aroused considerable interest in archaeological circles. Not that the genes in my pool were in need of much stimulation. They appeared to be insane. They were totally shameless. It's a shame, looking back, that all this came to an end so soon. It's also a pity that shame had to play a part in ending a cheery, if somewhat exhausting period.

The problem was simple. I was receiving mixed messages on the body and the spirit fronts.

First, 'He' made me, including presumably the genes that were now giving me grief. Second, because of my gene trouble, I'd recently learned I was going to have to clock-in for a ritual called confession. This was in order to apologize for the sin of sullying the me 'He'd' made. This seemed a bit harsh, but, 'yes, all right, Mum'.

Then there was the Adam and Eve problem.

They were part of the creation myth. But no one, none of the priests or nuns, or Mum, or anybody else I spoke to, believed they were actually real. You probably know the story better than I do, but as I recall, it went something like this:

Adam and Eve were an item who lived in a garden.

Adam was the first human being God made. Then 'He' made Eve, Adam's wife, out of Adam's rib. In the garden was a tree, the tree of the knowledge of good and evil. Adam was told, don't eat the apples. Adam disobeyed. Adam and Eve sinned. They fell from grace into sin. And you, me and all human beings were considered to have sinned at that same moment. All humans, as a result of Adam's disobedience, are born guilty of sin because of our descent from Adam.

Smashing story, highly inventive, but it was easy to see why no one believed it.

'Mum, if nobody believes in Adam and Eve, why do we need a redeemer?'

'Shut up and eat your grits.'

There was more.

This hand-me-down sin of Adam's wasn't the only sin. There was one that came our way before Adam took the apple. This was the original sin, the one we're all born with. This is the sin that causes us to make sinful choices, think sinful thoughts, and feel sinful feelings.

Well, something was doing it. I could vouch for that.

But, Mum, if nobody believes the Adam and Eve story...?

'Grits!'

Actually, there was a lot of gritting going on at this time, mainly of my teeth.

The confession lark they'd signed me up for was purgatorial. I thought I was red faced when buying my course work from Mr. Davis. This was nothing to the cochineal mask I wore in the confessional. The whole thing was ghastly. There was one priest at the Servites, Father Jensen, who was kind to me and I liked him. It would be unbearable if he were behind the grille! The grille, by the way, was a wire mesh affair that divided you from the priest in the confessional box. If you leaned back it looked like the priest was covered in netting. Or was that because I had netting on my mind?

It makes me squirm to think about it, but for a while, this was the routine.

Go on the roof. Study. Go to heaven. Come down. Go to hell. No wonder I was going to pieces. If every time you went to heaven you had to go and see Father Jensen, forget it. It was probably wearing him out as well as me. I hardly had the strength to climb the drainpipes. It couldn't last and it didn't. In an attempt to regain some self-respect, I gave up confession. All this embarrassment was inflicted, so I was told, in order to keep my soul in good working order.

That reminds me, we never decided when the soul actually came aboard, did we.

Have you ever heard of Gregory of Nyssa? Neither had I. In the 4th century he wrote extensively on the subject in an essay called, On the Soul and the Resurrection.

I put the question to a few classmates but their replies were inconclusive to say the least. Pepper was baffled. Croft likewise. Seabrook had never heard of souls. Bishop, despite his name, thought you got them at the fishmonger.

As for Bushell, was it worth asking?

This star, who was in my class, was famed throughout all the primary and secondary schools of west London for his prowess and exploits in certain, shall we say, delicate matters. He had taken a different road to self-knowledge. He was totally without inhibition, an attitude that, with commendable entrepreneurial skill, he had turned into a nice little earner. Tall, thin and lanky, he was in one respect awesomely well built and did not mind who knew it.

The scam he profited from was simple.

Sat at his desk, with the lid up to act as a screen, he could when his personhood was in the right frame of mind, place upon its end the screw top cap of a Stephen's ink bottle. Then, bending things to his will, he would release his mighty machine. Under the immense energy liberated, the cap would fly upwards and strike the ceiling of classroom 5B.

Of course, I don't expect you to believe this.

Why should you? No one else did, certainly none of his fellow scholars. They would bet it couldn't be done. Bushell would accept the bet. Down went their pocket money. A time would be arranged, up would go the desk lid, and off would

143

come the ink bottle top. The astonishing deed would be done and away would slink another fleeced youth, his pockets emptied, his manhood diminished.

No, I didn't ask Bushell. He was probably as far from Gregory of Nyssa on the subject as one could get.

I consulted my cereal packs again and found:

'Ensoulment has been asserted to occur in the sperm before conception; at conception; at the time a mother can feel the foetus within her; at birth; or even later. Different religions have different views. The Catholic Church's Magisterium says the moment the human zygote - the fertilized egg - is formed, it possesses potentiality and actuality and is ensouled. That's why the church condemns any type of procured abortion as tantamount to murder. If a zygote has the potential to become human, so has an unfertilized egg. And so has sperm. An average male ejaculation contains hundreds of millions of sperm cells. And, oddly, although the Old and New Testaments contain nothing about prohibiting abortion, pro-lifers say abortion is tantamount to murder. So, is masturbation mass murder?'

Stone me! Mass murder! I was in deeper than I thought.

If I confessed to mass murder along at the Servites there'd be hell to pay. It would be a severe blow to Father Jensen's ministry. Think of the penance I'd have to do! I'd be forever hailing the mistranslation.

144

There was another thing. Some energetic pro-lifers include Hitler, Stalin, Mussolini and Ceausescu, a grisly quartet with whom I do not care to associate. Adolescence is a puzzling time. Maybe I should have prayed for guidance. Maybe I would if I hadn't come across Sir Francis Galton. He was one of Britain's earliest speculative scientists. He had published, in 1872, Statistical Inquiries into the Efficacy of Prayer. His findings were that prayer didn't work. On publication there was hell to pay! His work, of course, is ignored in our fundamentalist times. Yet I tended to agree with Sir Francis. I'd prayed long and hard to not have to go to church or school and that hadn't worked.

But if doubts reigned on the supernatural front, help was at hand biologically.

This was the only exception to my sex education being left up to me. One day I was lying idly on my bed in my room. Have you read War and Peace? It's a big book. It is as nothing to the tome that was now added to my library. To this day I'm convinced no one knew I was in the room. What happened was this. My bed was behind the door. The door flew open, a huge book was lobbed in the direction of the bed, and the door shut again.

The book landed like a paving stone, corner first, on the front of my left hip. Two inches to the right and we would not be discussing this subject. It was a textbook on biology, full of the dance of the chromosomes. I danced about like a chromosome for the joy of receiving it.

In the right light, you can still see the dinge in my hip.

Chapter XXII
The life class.

There were no life classes at Sloane. It was a disappointingly nipple-free zone. But there were art classes. As a painter, I am self-taught. That means, as someone pointed out, you've been taught by an incompetent amateur. True, up to a point. But in a way, there were several teachers.

Uncle Jack - of the Auntie Win and Uncle Jack double-act - was an early pedagogue in this department. He was yet another uncle of my early days whom I loved unreservedly. Jack Martin was, I believe, some sort of construction engineer or road gang worker. He frequented the public bar of the Sun, when he had the opportunity, which wasn't often. Sometimes, if Uncle Jack was in the party, I'd be allowed to sit in among the road gang at the public bar's 12-seater table. This was the grown-up's world writ large. The gentlemen of the company were, for the most part, built on the same floor plan as Pat Brady. Dominoes disappeared into massive fists, emerging folded and crumpled from the heat of battle. Pints of Guinness were held like thimbles between formidable fingers. The talk was of uprooted roads and uprooted lives. Giant forearms, tanned and tattooed, lay like logs at rest on the public pine. Austerity was the word of the day. Nothing was wasted. Matches flared and lit Woodbines, then picked at mighty molars, then served to mark the state of play on timeworn cribbage boards.

'Fifteen-two, fifteen-four, fifteen-six, fifteen-eight and one for his knob!'

Uncle Jack and I go back a long way. He passed me many a tin bath when the Luftwaffe was about. And when they'd gone and we emerged into the light, if there was a light still working, he was one of the relatives who always seemed to have time to spare for me. Our favourite game was drawing. I'd sit on his lap and be trusted with the coloured crayons.

We always drew the same picture. I call it an Uncle-Jack-Scape.

I'll describe it but feel free to draw along with me. Take a sheet of A4 paper, portrait way up. From a quarter of the way down the left edge, draw a curving line down to the bottom edge, about a quarter way in from the right. Now, from about a third of the way down the page, draw a horizontal line from the curve to the right edge of the paper. That horizontal line is the horizon of the sea. What sea? Well, look at what you've just drawn. You've defined three areas. The top is sky. Below that to the right is the sea. And to the left is the great cliff top of land. In the sky, draw a roundel of sun, about the size of a slice of one of Mum's hard-boiled eggs. Then from lower down on the curve, draw out into the water a small wooden jetty with a rowing boat moored to it. Add a few squiggles of reflection in the water, put a tree or two on the cliff top and a couple of tiny double curves in the sky for seagulls. Finally, colour it in. Now write the date in the top right corner, and then sign it at the bottom right.

Good, isn't it.

When I win the lottery, I might endow an annual Uncle-Jack-Scape competition open to all comers. The pictures must all be of the same scene. Prizes will be awarded for the paintings that most evoke the pleasure one kindly construction engineer gave a small kid in the long ago.

Who knows, the Uncle-Jack-Scape competition might not be all I'd endow. There could also be the Uncle-Jack-Portrait competition. We didn't draw a lot of portraits, but he did show me a game that removes any trepidation anyone might have about drawing a likeness. If you have children - of any age - I urge you to force this upon them.

Get a few people together, maybe the family sitting round a table that has a tablecloth. Give everyone a pencil and paper. Ask them to put the pencil and paper on their knee, out of sight under the tablecloth. Then invite them to draw anyone at the table they choose. The point being, they can't see the drawing they're making. Neither can anyone else. They mustn't say whom they're drawing. The game is to guess who they have drawn.

To begin with everybody says: 'I can't do this, I can't draw.'

What that means, of course, is not that they can't draw, but that they don't draw.

The results are always, shall we say, surprising and nearly always maniacally funny. What is remarkable, is no matter how disconnected the drawings are, the sitters are usually recognizable. All these people who 'can't draw', suddenly produce likenesses, mad likenesses maybe, but likenesses none the less.

How?

Simple. Because they can't see what they're drawing, they don't worry about the artwork. They concentrate, not on producing a 'good' drawing, but on looking, seeing, observing. That's the secret. As they look, they search for what is distinctive. Long hair, bald heads, beards, spectacles, clothes, whatever.

Uncle Jack not only drew, he also played vamp piano in the saloon bar. He encouraged me to play. The subsequent results are no reflection on his talent.

The art classes at Sloane were only one surprising thing about the school.

The most surprising thing was there were two other boys there with the same surname as mine. They were cousins, from the 'vultures' side of the family. One was older than me, one younger, both never seen since. Homonym the Younger had red hair. Homonym the Elder was clever, able, athletic and politically shrewd. He captained the first eleven at cricket and went on to captain the school. Then, in a flash of political skill, he appointed me as a Monitor. This rank was less than a Prefect, but a step up from the common herd.

At a stroke I was neutered, my antics curtailed.

Swearing me in as one of his lieutenants involved the briefest ceremony. Sloane pupils enjoyed, from time to time, what were called spare periods, lessons when no master was available. During these periods, you revised, did homework and were generally full of self-disciplined diligence. It was during such a period that my elevation came.

At the time of my appointment, I was lying flat out across the absent master's desk, engrossed in a game of two penny-halfpenny football. This sport involves two penny players and sixpenny ball. You hit the pennies with a comb. They in turn hit the sixpence and you attempt to score by shooting the tanner through goals at each end of the desk. The goals are made of further pairs of pennies set a regulation distance apart. My classmates were lolling around, idly betting on the game and mulling over their futures, when the door opened and suddenly the School Captain was among us.

'You,' he said to me, 'are appointed as a School Monitor.'

He handed me a lapel badge, turned, went out and I never spoke to him again.

That was that. I was astonished. I was already 3-1 down and now my concentration was ruined. Not to mention my reputation. I looked around the room. Pepper was baffled. Croft likewise. Seabrook had never heard of Monitors. Bishop, as usual, thought they came from the fishmonger. But we're getting ahead of ourselves. My promotion wasn't until much later. Here we are discussing education - the early years.

In my first term Sloane School seemed a strange place. For example, I'd never seen a fives court before. In fact, I'd never seen a fours court, a threes court, a twos court, or a ones court, let alone a fives court. I'd been to Earl's Court, of course, but that didn't count.

The assembly hall had an imposing raised stage, a large lectern, side pillars, and in the background above the stage, you could see the gallery that ran round three sides of the hall. If you were seated to the left, near the Hortensia Road windows, you could just see, up on the gallery the door to classroom 5B where Bushell performed his miracles and ran the Tote.

Off the assembly hall, opposite the windows, and sharing the same polished parquet floor, was the school library with its endless stacks of purpose-built wooden shelving. You entered the library through imposing double doors. At one end of this hushed and hallowed space was a long shelf filled entirely with copies of Punch magazine in red leather binders. How sophisticated was that? So sophisticated, that the youth, the down gone from his chin, would one day start his own collection and fill shelves in his own residence, binders and all. The collection grew and grew until, on another day, the scales fell from his eyes and he put the lot in a domestic-sized skip hired from Grundons Waste Management of Wallingford, Oxon, £111.63 including VAT.

Below the assembly hall was the school gym, a huge area around which we were hunted in packs by a series of red and black striped pullover-wearing gym teachers. The Master of Hounds was Mr Ind. Off the gym were the changing rooms. It was there, a year or two later a lout twice my size and three years older, handed me the mandatory school beating up. I can't recall his name, only the bolt through his neck. I trust an early doom befell him along with Jack of Kinsbourne Green Primary.

Physical education, PE, was not a favourite lesson.

Of course, favouritism should play no part in education. Teaching must be even handed. Not that there was any risk of my becoming anyone's favourite. To the teaching faculty it was soon clear I was not the loam in which the sower of knowledge seeks to plant the seed. I was evidently stony ground on legs, definitely not the row to hoe. I attribute the source of this slander to the school nurse. She'd been heard to say if my ears were syringed the water would hose straight through. I resented this slur, but it helped my cause. Invisibility became my aim. I worked hard at staying off everyone's radar. One way to do this was to work hard even if you got nowhere. So that's what I did.

Physics was another no-no.

Of the boundless wonders of the physical world I knew little. To my regret, I know little more now than when I first beheld the blazing Bunsen burners. I recall nothing of the subject except, in almost eidetic detail, the top floor classroom where we were introduced to electromagnetism in its most accessible form, electricity. The nameless tutor - he had a name but it escapes me and here's why - had wired up an elaborate apparatus. I do not claim for one moment to be psychic but I knew, at a glance, this branch of the tree of life was not for me. On one end of the high bench was a 12-volt car battery, at the other end sat a Leyden jar, laden with the pickled remains of earlier pupils. The teacher lined up his victims in a semicircular arc in front of the bench. He explained the plot, plausibly drawing us into covenant with him. He asked the two wingmen to hold one end each of the contraption. They grasped the wires. The other pupils were invited to join hands with the celebrants on either side of them. We did so, linking ourselves in a continuous, trusting loop. The master then threw a switch and shot an instructive bolt of lightning through the arc of the covenant. I was told later this was entirely legal and in America furniture manufacturers made chairs in this style. The result was profound. With one accord we leaped like sockeye salmon broaching the falls to spawn. Mike Oaktree, to his credit, coughed, spluttered and started up like a lawn mower. It took the school nurse - Nurse Slander as I called her -some time to switch him off. The event forever put me off shaking hands and ruined my prospects of a career in the *corps diplomatique.*

I recorded Physics: 0 on my scorecard, signed it and handed it in at the clubhouse.

Chemistry, too, found little favour with me.

I attended closely but somehow it all seemed to gather into a cloud and waft by. There was partly due to my sense of smell. My nose had taken an unusual beating for one so young, what with inhaling concentrated doses of incense, the fumes of a million devotional candles, and Dur-Dur's roof garden at its ripest. Some of the 'obnoxious effluvias' in chemistry felled boys built like oxen. Despite this, we were encouraged to toy with elements that fizzed, flamed, froze, sparkled, spat, glowed or exploded. Some of them, to our enchantment, did these things when they were supposed to.

Even so, reluctantly, once again I had to mark the scorecard: Chemistry: 0.

Wood and metalworking fared no better.

I'm all for reading, writing, and wroughting (wrought: *Metallurgy*. shaped by hammering or beating) except that things wrought by me tended not to come out wrought as they ought, if you follow me. These classes often resulted in my hands - and sometimes most of my bodily person - being covered in welts, cuts, bruises and blood blisters. To acquire these blisters, all you need is a vice with a long, heavy steel handle that slides through a socket to close the jaws of the machine. If you allow the handle to slip so the bolt-head top slams on to that loose flap of flesh twixt your forefinger and thumb - 'the abductor pollicis' according to Nurse Slander - the result is a blood blister.

This common accident was usually followed by the maximum opening of your own jaws as you passed news of the event to your fellow wroughters. Similar damage could be inflicted to fingers, thumbs and other body parts by saws, mallets, hammers and other readily available weaponry. Despite the carnage, pupils were encouraged to pursue their studies until proficient, expelled or dead.

Wroughting, noughting, in my view.

So was nothing right? Did nothing or nobody get ten-out-of-ten for teaching in these tender years? Cometh the hour, cometh the man. Step into the limelight and take a bow, Mr Smart, art master. He was large, tweedy and moustached. Mr Smart

156

was amiable, affable and under his tutelage his subject took on qualities I liked and responded to. He ruled without a rod. He was a big man, so big no discipline was needed because nobody larked about. You did more or less what you liked. What I liked most was daydreaming. And if daydreaming, with a pencil in your hand isn't part of art, I don't know what is.

Mr. Smart's world was calm, tranquil, enjoyable and fun. Of Mr. Smart's teaching I recall only thing. But what a thing! One Homeric, Herculean, Olympian, Apollonian diktat that will live on down the years, until the 'last syllable of recorded time'.

One of the regular art lessons was called, Free Composition. This was exactly what it says on the tin. You were free to draw and paint whatever you liked. So what did the Sloane sophisticates take for their subject? Why, the prevailing Zeitgeist, of course.

War.

I admit, for two terms I thought the Zeitgeist was a German fighter plane. As a result a good many Zeitgeist 109s, trailing smoke and flame, had been consigned to the ocean deep in my pictures.

I was good at war. Leaning on my early exposure to mutilation and butchery, I peopled my war-scapes liberally with lifelike - deathlike - associations of soldiers, sailors and airmen. Spitfires spat fire, bullets traced arcs across calamitous skies, bombs burst, shell holes gaped, barbed wire coiled, cities smouldered, shards of shrapnel filled the air, broken trees stood stark on blasted heaths, Panzers prowled the plains, Tiger tanks tore earth to trackless wastes, torpedoes surged, U-boats sank brave allied ships like sitting ducks, battleships battled, destroyers destroyed, shipwrecked souls swam in seas of burning oil, not waving, not drowning, frying.

Ah, happy days.

Around the class would come Mr. Smart, this Cenotaph of a man, quietly and calmly offering help and advice. He'd peer over your shoulder at the gore-soaked scene, carefully considering its composition. He would then point to some battle zone where perhaps the casualties were thin upon the ground.

'You've got a bit of a gap there, my boy. Why not put in a bit of bush?'

Bit of bush!

Forget Kenneth Clark. Step aside, E.H. Gombrich. On your bike, Brian Sewell. Who could compete with this?

Mr Smart said the same thing to everyone, irrespective of the scene, war or peace. It became his nickname, he became known as 'bit of bush'.

No wonder I love art.

The mad thing is, it worked! I would often put in a bit of bush (still do) and it cheered things up no end. Mind you, I always booby-trapped the shrub.

Chapter XXIII
A life in pictures.

Why I wonder, in these times past telling, was it Aunt Ethel who always took me to the pictures? For she it certainly was. I don't recall ever going to the cinema with Mum, certainly never with Uncle Reg. It was always Aunt Ethel who lugged me along to The Regal, The Forum, The Odeon, The Red Hall and other palaces of pleasure. I loved these outings. Without them The Wizard of Oz would never have terrified me witless. For some reason, the Tin Man in that film induced a kind of seizure in the infant seated in the 1/9ds. To ease his suffering and that of the audience we were, to Aunt Ethel's shame, escorted from the premises by the St John's Ambulance Brigade. Not all of them, just one or two. We took with us the scorn of many Chelsea Pensioners and the other afternoon cineastes at The Forum, Fulham Road.

On happier occasions, for me if not for Aunt Ethel, I recall swinging like an ape from her hand, yodelling all the way home to the pub - giving a special evolutionary whoop as we passed the Servite Church - having been transfixed by the adventures of 'me-Tarzan-you-Jane-him-Cheetah'. An afternoon spent in the jungles of Hollywood could incite in the next generation a desire to shin up the soil pipes to the canopy of his rain forest in record time.

At some cinemas, the films were augmented by live entertainment. This came in the form of the deadliest torture known to mankind. Just as you'd settled back to watch Tarzan's Jane slither down a sapling in something skimpy, a gent wearing a sequinned jacket, would levitate up through the floor seated at the world's worst musical instrument, an electric organ. I was surprised these were legal. They were as loud as doodlebugs. They were weapons of mass ear hole destruction. One e-flat could melt a choc-ice at a hundred paces. What misery cinemagoers had inflicted on the Musician's Union for them to take such revenge I do not know. Usherettes were known to stick torches in their ears during recitals. Some people, used to air raids no doubt, were even said to enjoy the din. Organ bombardments lasted at least twenty-minutes which flew past like twenty-years. At last, just when you were hoping the ground would open up and swallow you, the ground would open up and swallow the organist, sequins and all. Relief was tempered by the feeling of outrage. If J.S. Bach himself, in sequins, had arisen and given us the Toccata and Fugue in D

Minor he would still have got the bird. Like a Zeitgeist 109, he would have gone down in a hail of peanuts.

One cinema we were allowed to visit without aunts, was the Saturday morning sixpenny rush at The Broadway, Walham Green. This cinema was known as the fleapit. That wasn't its official title. That was what fleas called it. The fleapit was an auditorium in a condemned shed-like building. It would have been demolished long ago but the demolition workers union had forbidden their members to go near it. The Luftwaffe wouldn't bomb it for fear of reprisals. This no-go area was reached by way of the arcade leading to Walham Green Underground station. This station, later renamed Fulham Broadway, is served by the District Line. This is a semi-organic, slug-like arrangement that crawls around under the stones of London. The District Line was old when Methuselah was young.

The tanner rush on a Saturday morning had a keen following. Everyone went there to try to catch polio, which was all the rage at the time. Polio could be fatal. It could induce paralysis. But it guaranteed time off school. Well worth the risk. You had to be searched before you went in. You were only allowed in if you had a knife or a razor. There was an immense stampede when the doors opened at 10 am as the tribes raced for the few seats still waiting to be slashed.

The films were great. We hated them all. We hated Roy Rogers and Trigger as they spangled about on the back lots of

Los Angeles. We hated The Bowery Boys and The Dead End Kids. We hated Laurel and Hardy and watched them every week. We hated 'Ke-mo sah-bee, what's this? A fiery horse with the speed of light, a cloud of dust and a hearty, Hi-Yo, Silver, Away! The Lone Ranger Rides Again!'

We enjoyed the finest cinema the age could offer: comedy, drama, film noir, continental, Les Stooges Trois. We had a lot of film noir because the projector often broke. There were three versions of projector breakdown.

The first was: 'Yahh! Booo! Why are we waiting?' Click, film restarts, 'Hooray!'

The second was: 'Yahh! Booo! Why are we waiting?' followed by the house lights coming on and the United Nations - or was it The League of Nations - coming in to separate warring factions, 'Boo-oo!'

The third version was all the above, followed by the exit doors opening because the back wall of the building had fallen off, taking with it in its flight one projector, two projectionists, three St. John's Ambulance ladies and half the seed of Europe.

We couldn't wait for next week. It was bound to be better.

In The Wizard of Oz, the Tin Man scared me. In the jungle, I was scared of no one. In the Broadway, Walham Green, if you had any sense, you were scared of the patrons. But the real scare came in the Odeon cinema in Colchester.

That's where we saw, on Pathé news, the atom bomb go off. I was on holiday and had been taken to the pictures by some or all of the Porter girls, Celia, Patricia, Kitty, Winnie and Peggy. The horror of Hiroshima was beyond us. We'd be next, we knew it, but we weren't, Nagasaki was. The immensity of the devastation, the scale of it was petrifying. But the undying image was the strangeness of the dying. The ghastly, ghostly pictures of the few surviving wretches moving, as if in slow motion, naked but with the shadows of chairs and patterns of curtains burnt onto the skin of their very bodies. How could shadows become branded on to people? How could this be? We went home in a changed mood.

It didn't stop us going to the pictures, of course.

On another occasion the same team smuggled me into to see a movie I wish the British Board of Film Censors had kept to themselves. This was a noir-y sort of thriller that gave me nightmares for years afterwards. It was about a man who was trying to kill a woman, and she was in some sort of home, and he got over the wall, and he had a long knife, and this knife had a wavy edge to the top of the blade and a wavy edge on the other edge of the blade, and the film was in black and white, and the music went thud-thud-thud, and I couldn't bear to look, and Celia, Patricia, Kitty, Winnie and Peggy and everyone else screamed all at the same time, and it was nearly as noisy as the flea pit but with grown-ups making the noise and I can't remember the name of the film but an actor called John Hodiak was in it.

Cinema began to lose its appeal. I regularly turned up at the box office sound in wind and limb and came out wrecked. Unknown to me, yet another cinema would soon enter my list of picture palaces to avoid. This was in far away Scotland.

With a surname like mine, Scotland was inevitably sprinkled with folk claiming kinship. One of these was mystery Aunt Kate of Old Cumnock.

As the endless expanse of one school summer holiday spread ahead of them, Mum and Reg saw the opportunity of broadening the child's mind by sending him to Scotland. It was like the nuns and the roundabout at the Marist Convent all over again. I was suckered into it, life having taught me nothing, by the irresistible prospect of the train journey north. Come on, be fair, The Royal Scot, 6100, out of Euston, the water troughs at Watford Junction, any kid in his right mind would have said yes. Uncle Reg was so keen on the idea he offered to escort me. And, sure, he could get tickets, no problem.

Bye Mum, bye Marg, bye Dur-Dur, I was gone.

In the toilet of the third-class, Glasgow-bound LMS coach, liveried in red, gold and grime, carefully scratched in the polished wood were the words:

'No matter how much you shake your peg, the last three drops run down your leg.'

Although it was unsigned, I was enchanted. How could anyone be so wise? This was not my first brush with poetry. But this was clearly on a more elevated plain than: 'There's a cupboard under the stairs....' and other juvenilia. This was the true power of literature, the Elysian Fields themselves, just south of Hemel Hempstead.

I thought about this as, back in my seat, I dried off.

Change trains at Glasgow Central, on to Kilmarnock; change again, then to Old Cumnock, all by steam train. Magic. It took about a week.

Mystery Aunt Kate was an elderly body who lived in a white painted, thatched roofed cottage, with a low door. Inside was dark. I was involved in a welcome-to-the-wee-laddie conversation but I never actually met the lady. She remained a mystery. We were billeted some distance away, with friendly folk who lived in a magic house, right by a level crossing. By a level crossing! Boy, they sure knew how to live in those parts. The trains came to you! Uncle Reg stayed for a day or two and then escaped. I think my hosts had offspring of my age, but I'm not sure.

What I am sure of is I saw some eye-opening sights.

I was taken to watch a professional football game in Kilmarnock. We joined the crowd walking up the hill to the pitch that was on a raised plateau. The spectators, at least the ones where we were, were lower than pitch, on eye level with the player's boots. This was odd enough. But, even odder, it was here I found out why many Scotsmen of this era were, how should we put it, vertically challenged. The pitch was made of cinders. I mean lumps of coke, off-cuts from the local Gas, Light & Coke Company. The players were being abraded, sandpapered down from the legs up as we watched. They were losing height before our very eyes. It wasn't just eye opening, it was knee-opening, elbow-opening and, if you happened to fall on your face, well, if you don't want to know the result, look away now please.

And as for the Old Cumnockians' outdoor swimming pool, that was astounding.

It was set in a wonderful wooded valley. The pool can't be there any longer. European Human Rights legislation wouldn't allow it. The diving board tower was a hazard to passing aircraft even then. A local McSherpa took me to the top. Looking down, which wasn't advisable, you could - on a clear day - see the pool below. I was told Scottish persons dived into the water from here. I didn't. I climbed down. And, then, as if I hadn't suffered enough, they took me to the pictures.

Like their counterparts in the kindly south, the bravehearts looked forward to their Saturday morning sixpenny rush. I rushed along with them. The excited crowd queued and scrummed before the gates were opened and in we surged, keen as ever to collar the unslashed seats.

166

More surprises for the Sassenach.

There were no unslashed seats. There were no slashed seats. There were no seats.

'Noo,' was the courteous reply to my enquiry. 'We dunna have nae seats, we mak doo wi' the concrete, it soots us fine.'

Despite Mum having served in India, I found there was little of the Gunga Din about me in the matter of sitting cross-legged on the cold concretes of the Cumnocks, Old or New. There was, however, one final joy to be relished during my airing in Ayrshire.

That was the matter of the signal box. Naturally, as you would expect, I gravitated towards the nearby railway line. This, joy of joys, was the main line. That meant expresses! That meant Royal Scots! The line ran along the side of a majestic, billowing sweep of hills. Away to the left - the north - was a long, endless straight of converging track before, almost at the limit of vision, the by-now-miraging steel disappeared behind trees. To the right - the south - the sight line was almost as long but curved gracefully in a long left-hander before the ample foothills once again clasped it to their bosom.

This magnificent cinemascope vista of all that was worth living and collecting numbers for, meant every passing train, even a thunderous, hurtling express would be visible almost horizon to horizon, almost as long as sight would allow. There was no station here, just one lone signal box. This was perfection.

It was the Hangar straight at Silverstone, Eau Rouge at Spa, the Mulsanne at Le Mans; it was harry flatters, full chat, pedal to the metal all the way. This was the summit, the pinnacle, the very Everest of train spotting. And it was all-mine, all-mine!

And, faint to tell, there was more to come.

The signal box, which was this side of the tracks, was built like a tall cottage. It had a panoramic glasshouse top floor and an outside wooden stairway. One day I was, as usual, hanging around waiting for distant steam whistles to summon me to my lookout post by the fence, when the signalman saw me and said hello. This was astonishing. I was used to being invited to hoppit by brother officers of the London, Midland & Scottish Railway. There was more astonishment to come. The signalman wasn't a signalman but a signal woman! She asked if I'd like a cup of tea. Speechless nod. She asked me if I'd like to drink the tea in the holy of holies, the glass fronted box itself. Speechless nod, climb the wooden stairs, consciousness gradually slipping away. And there they were. The long rows of polished levers, higher than me almost. The lamps. The lights. The switches. The tink of metal spoon in enamel mugs. Her explaining. Me listening, mouthing monosyllables.

Then suddenly, the bells! the bells!

From the south it came, distant at first but vibrant, pulsating, breasting the rise from the curve of the foothills, The Royal Scot itself with fifteen coaches, flat out, plumed in clouds of its own cumulus, breathing fire into the very sleepers, pounding and roaring in my ears, the shrieking whistle, one long then two short blasts of greeting, Doppler high, Doppler low as its awesome magnificence thundered past, the signal box itself shaking and rattling, the signal lady waving through the open window, the driver waving back, then the long run to the far converging curve until the rails themselves were all that was left, shimmering with intensity.

The boy stood on the burning deck.

He might just as well have done. What more could life offer now? I'd been there, done that, got the tea shirt. Literally. My cup, well, my enamel mug, had runneth over down my front. What of that!

Every waking moment from then on was spent, if possible, in the box. I ran errands, did little jobs. I was useful. I'd never been that before. It felt good but it couldn't last. All too soon my minders were back to collect me. Then came the final astonishment of my Celtic summer. We did the return journey the same way but in reverse order: Old Cumnock, Kilmarnock, Glasgow and so to Euston. It took about another week. But here was the killer. It happened on the first train, the local rattler from Old Cumnock. I wasn't mad about local trains. It was pulled by a steam engine all right, but I was mainlining even then. Mind you, I was still excited enough to need to go for a pee.

You've guessed.

On the wall in the toilet of the third-class, Kilmarnock-bound LMS coach, liveried in red, gold and grime, carefully scratched in the polished wood were the words:

'No matter how much you shake your peg, the last three drops run down your leg.'

It was the same coach! I was overwhelmed by the coincidence. Back in the compartment I sank into my seat.

'As we grow older the world becomes stranger.'

This was something to think about as I dried off.

Chapter XXIV
'Hi Jean!'

Thursdays were the best of my schooldays, the afternoons anyway.

We were paroled from Sloane at lunchtime. Swallow a few egg roundels at home, and then catch a Number 14 bus to Putney Bridge. Change to a Number 30 and up the hill to the school sports ground at Roehampton. This vast swathe of green was the scene of some of the most spectacular defeats and idiocies in sporting legend. It wasn't just me who was hopeless. We all shared in the glory.

I didn't break records, I mainly broke bones.

One day, Uncle Reg came to watch me play football. Keen to impress I raced towards goal. Just then an especially aggressive tussock of turf sprang up before me. Snap! The sound of the left wrist breaking echoed across the prairie. This was followed by the howl of its owner calling for its mother. A kid called Lanky Dixon in form 3A was double-jointed but even he couldn't do what my wrist was doing at that moment. Six weeks in plaster, arm in sling. It itched like mad when it reappeared and the skin was all flaky.

But did this quench the spirit?

Or did fortitude kick in? Fortitude kicked in. Well, actually I think it was Harrison who kicked in. This was from the penalty spot on my first game back in the squad. I should never have played in goal. I can see that now. Unfortunately Harrison didn't see it that way. He kicked the ball straight at me. To protect myself, I held my arms straight out, hands up at right angles, palms forward.

Snap!

The sound of the same left wrist breaking again echoed across the prairie. The youth once again called for its maternal parent. Lanky Dixon, though interested, said he wasn't even going to attempt to do what my wrist was doing now. An odd look from the same bone-setting surgeon, six weeks in plaster, arm in sling and it itched even worse when it came out, the skin even flakier.

Despite these set backs our protégé was willing to play further afield. Hackney Marshes, on a frozen Sunday morning in early January, has never rivalled the Great Barrier Reef as a tourist magnet. Yet this wasteland regularly attracted Barbarian hordes.

Once again, I was in full flight, my footwork impressing the impresarios lining the touchline when yet another tussock turned up.

Snap!

It was the by now familiar sound of something personal reconfiguring. Hold up wrists for examination. Both still attached, but find I can't move head. Howl in vain for distant forebear. Walk, well limp, with odd twisted half-bent gait, two miles to nearest hospital, dragging kit bag.

'Prosthetics, first left, mate.'

Figure of eight bandage, collarbones, broken, for the use of.

'Take it off when it's better' said the doctor, 'and my advice is don't play again for a while.'

'My advice is never play again,' said his nurse, who'd been watching the match.

I rose above the slur. I'd had slurs from nurses before.

So to cricket.

This took place at Roehampton. Like everything else at Sloane, sports were well organised. Thursdays saw us field four teams: the first eleven, second eleven, third eleven and the catching practisers. I held a regular place in the latter, and, though I say it myself, I was good at catching. I should explain, in catching practice, the ball is thrown into a bent wood catching frame, it flies out at unexpected angles and you catch it. That's the theory. Little got past me. I'd had years of experience tormenting Mr Brown. I was youthful, nimble, almost agile every now and then. Then one day the call came to join the third eleven. The honour, the pride, the disaster.

173

We were fielding at the time.

One of the batsmen, a beefy sort of oaf, hit the ball towards me. Cricket is all about timing. By some fluke the oaf had timed the shot perfectly. A cricket ball when well struck can achieve ballistic velocities. The perfectly timed shot, shot towards me and unimpeded may have reached Stamford Bridge if not Hackney Marshes. The third eleven, well ten of them, called to their newest team member to catch it. He heard the shouts but he also heard something else. The ball as it approached was making a loud, whirring, threatening noise. In its own way, it was saying: don't even think about it, mate. To my shame, I took its advice. I pretended to grab it but deliberately missed. I thought my cowardice would never be forgiven. But it was forgotten in an instant.

With the next ball a gloriously bloody accident occurred and, hooray, not to me.

My missed catch had been the last ball of the over. With the change of ends I was now fielding at third slip. On came our fastest bowler, renowned for his vicious bouncers. I was standing well back behind the wicket keeper. He was wearing big leg pads, big protective gloves and - his only sartorial mistake - his glasses. The bouncer reared up, missed the batsman's head by a whisker and hit the wicket keeper on the bridge of his nose precisely where sat his spectacles. The keeper went down, the glass went up. It looked for all the world like a splash of water in the afternoon sunlight. It wasn't only water that splashed upwards. There was blood everywhere. The kid writhed and moaned. We rushed to help. I rushed to thank him for wiping out my ignominy. We took turns to haul slivers of spectacle from his ample face. Amazingly, he could still see from both eyes. In fact, the blow appeared to have cured his astigmatism.

Mr. Ind, the games master appeared.

'Why on earth were you wearing glasses keeping wicket?' he said.

'Please, Sir, I can't see the ball without glasses,' moaned the wretch.

'You evidently can't see it with them,' said Mr. Ind.

Quite a good reply that I thought, witty you know, if a bit lacking in sympathy.

By now, as various games masters had noted, anthropologically speaking, I was more gracile than robust. If one was to have a purpose in life, it seemed to me self-preservation might as well be it. I therefore made a mental note: one, don't keep goal; two, don't keep wicket.

Actually, Mr Ind wasn't a bad sort of bloke. I saw quite a lot of him in casualty down the years. Our next meeting also involved cricket, but we have to back track to get the full story. Sloane was not the only school to grace Hortensia Road. Moored next to it was Carlyle Grammar School for Girls.

Hundreds of them, all corralled together, unthinkable. They shared the Roehampton playing fields with Sloane School. By coincidence, on Thursdays, a few score of them were let out on licence to play hockey. Carlyle Girls hockey was like Aussie rules football played by convicts. It was all short skirts and massive fractures. Well worth watching.

Watching was exactly what I was doing one fine day while fielding on the boundary in a needle game of cricket. The boundary, by happy chance, was next to the girl's pitch. Though I was engrossed in the cricket, it was difficult to ignore the whisper of white thighs behind me as they thundered about the heavy going. It was while lost in such a reverie I became aware of distant hollering from my team-mates.

'Oi! Catch it!'

I took no notice. A pack of the skirted savages had just cornered a quarry and were giving her what for in no uncertain terms, when....

At this point the lights went out.

Trajectories are interesting, don't you think? Isaac Newton worked them all out. Things go up, run out of steam, stop going up and start coming back down. The apple fell on his head, clarity dawned and the laws of motion were solved. A Granny Smith landing on Isaac's head may have helped the cause of calculus, but a cricket ball plunging into your parting from on high does little to advance science. Or cricket.

I didn't see stars.

When I finally opened my eyes I saw a complete circle of team-mates looking down at me. They formed a pattern like the petals of a sunflower. In the centre of the bloom appeared the face of Mr. Ind.

'You again,' he said in disbelief.

He waved a finger in front of my face. The last rites I thought, ace-king-queen-jack.

'Look at my finger,' he said, waving it from side to side to ascertain whether to call an ambulance or a hearse.

Later, going home on the Number 30, the lump on my head was so big I couldn't wear my school cap. Despite my distress, I forced myself to follow my Thursday ritual. By the bus stop at Putney bridge, where I changed to the Number 14, was a milk bar. Milk bars were American style cafés, all flashy chrome, spot lights, tall counters and high stools, much frequented by the in crowd. There had been a rival establishment, the Black & White Milk Bar, over the way, just past the Odeon. It had taken a direct hit during an air raid with shocking loss of life. My poison was a Pepsi-Cola served in a tall, chilled, state-of-the-art glass, with a scoop of vanilla ice cream and two straws. A Pepsi float it was called, yum yum, the high point of my week.

I would perch on the high stool, Edward Hopper style, toying with my tipple Bogart fashion, using the straws to dunk the ice cream to the bottom of the glass then letting it bounce to the surface. Wipe splash from face and repeat, while trying to blot out the pain in my head. The café was called the Hi Jean!

As I dunked, the name caught my eye. Hi Jean!

Hygiene!

It was my first pun. God knows, it wouldn't be my last, as any poor suffering soul who has stayed with me this far well knows.

The Hi Jean! has a lot to answer for.

Chapter XXV
The big E.

'Go on, Dud, you go first. I'll hold the bikes.'

'No, I'll hold them. I don't mind, really 'No, honest, you go.'

'No, no, after you Claude.'

Dudley and I were gentlemen to a fault especially where danger was concerned. And one of our enterprises did entail some light risk. The venue was the used tyre dump, below the Scrubs Lane bridge over the Grand Union canal and the Great Western railway line at Old Oak Common. It was irresistible. It contained all the essentials of the yet-to-be-invented trampoline. There was an abundance of elasticated material. On any given day there were several million unwanted inner tubes and tyres in stock. They were stacked up to the buttress of the bridge. In the corner to the left, you could almost step on to them from the parapet. They curved down from the left in a hill of sloping rubber. Away to the right, they were so far below you'd need a parachute to land on them safely. Who said anything about safely?

To reach the parapet you leant your bike against the wall, climbed on to the crossbar and stepped up to the dizzying height, which didn't look dizzying until you got there. The view was magnificent, uplifting. You could see Wormwood Scrubs prison and the catacombs at Kensal Rise cemetery. To complete this manoeuvre the bike must be held and steadied. There was stiff competition for the honour of holding the bike. The game was to see how high you'd dare jump from. The further to the right, the longer the drop.

We did some dummy runs at the shallow end. It was wonderfully spongy. The inner tubes were still inflated so you bounced about hilariously, coming to rest you knew not where. As you moved to the right, in increments of bicycle lengths - or Riddells - the longer the drop. I can't remember who made the first really big jump, probably not me. Also, I'm not sure at what point the rubber ceased to break your fall and broke your body. There was a definite point of criticality. I regret we didn't record the greatest height leapt. It would have been easy to calculate. Indeed, calculating it might have whiled away the long hours of convalescence. Another regret is we did it at all, suffering as I did with genuflector's knees.

The tubes and tyres were tipped on to the tip from the left. Each time we went there we found a new landscape, full of new challenges. In the tumble of tubes and tyres, it was how they came to rest that determined your injuries. Some days we'd find a placid sea of circles beckoning us to its bosom. On other days the sea was rougher, but we jumped anyway. The idea of the game was to see if we could make the following happen.

1. Somebody holds the bikes. 2. The other one leaps. 3. The leaper bounces up, his head appears over the parapet, he bids the bike holder good afternoon before plummeting back down. This never happened, at least not in the required order, 1, 2, and 3.

There are more hazards to trampolining than you may think. One of them was, in this postal district, you could easily land not on a trampoline, but on a tramp. There were many such gentlemen of the road inhabiting these environs, all of them anxious - and who can blame them - to not spill their methylated spirits. Another hazard concerned the laws of probability. No matter how often you toss a coin, the odds on it landing heads or tails are always one in two. But if you toss several million old inner tubes over a wall, the chances of some of them forming a chimney-like structure when they come to rest are more difficult to predict. But it can happen. On one occasion, the bike holder, concerned about the non-reappearance of the jumper, struggled up on to the parapet to have a look. There was no sign of his friend. There was no sign of anyone, not even a tramp. This was disturbing. Riding home with two bikes can be tricky. Distress noises were heard below. Slowly his companion emerged from just such a chimney. In the gathering twilight he squeezed his elbows on to the topmost tube and, looking for all the world like a lost meerkat, called in vain for a forebear.

Bikes, of course, were crucial to all enterprises. They were the only way we could escape civilisation. Mine was a Claude Butler, metallic pink, drop-handlebars, three-speed deraillier gears, Reynolds 531 tubing, dynamo lights and a racing saddle that sorely divided opinions. On the day I lost my no claims bonus, I was cruising home from Auntie Win and Uncle Jack's along Kelvedon Road. I'd recently mastered the art of riding without holding the handlebars and with my hands in my trouser pockets. Nonchalant, eh? I invited admiring looks, hoping there might be some golden haired lovely peeking out from behind lace curtains, her heart a-flutter at the sight of the mysterious stranger when … Wham!

I rode into the back of a parked car.

The devastation caused by a collision at nought miles an hour is surprising. The spot can be pinpointed. Kelvedon Road runs by the wall of the Marist Convent. That wall again! The one I'd slammed into a few years earlier, when leaving the magic roundabout. Coincidence? Spooky if you ask me. And where did that car come from suddenly? It was the only one parked in the road. Streets were like that then.

My Claude Butler - crossbar bent at right angles - and I, went home, not riding, not walking, limping and peering out through curtains of blood. Typical, where was Mr Ind when you needed him most?

Claude, the bike, was supposed to be kept in the cupboard under the stairs. But often I couldn't be bothered to put it away. If left out in the tiny hallway, the bike impeded the household. It caused congestion, anger and strife. Why didn't I put it away? Because the hated cupboard was low, and full of brooms and mops and buckets and other grown up toys of no use to a body. There were quantities of coats hung behind the door. Everything had to be moved out of the way to get the bike in. It drove me mad. So I often left the bike out and it drove everyone else mad. Sometimes though, if Big Pat Brady said put the bike away, it seemed to fit in easily. I still have ridges on my skull from the number of times I banged my head in that hellhole cupboard.

As for the stairs themselves, I had a special relationship with them.

I rarely descended them in the proscribed manner. Was it an argument over the bike that prompted Uncle Reg to throw me down a flight or two? I can't remember. I can remember how he did it. We were standing at the top, me with my back to the stairs, facing the hallstand. The ten-year old was enraged about something and kicked out wildly at the former professional footballer. The sportsman moved back and caught the heel of the kicking foot as it swung upwards. He lifted it slightly, tipping the kicker off balance and over backwards.

The stairs, I should explain, were a curious shape.

The last I saw of the hallstand on this occasion was when I bore left at the half-landing halfway down. Beyond that you went down one or two more steps before bearing left again, back on yourself as it were, still descending. Finally, a couple of steps from the end, you turned left once more before coming to a halt on the floor of the tiny hall where the bike shouldn't be parked. As I say, the stairs were a curious shape. By now, so was I.

I didn't kick over the traces again, but it was not the last time I fell down the stairs.

The next time I did so I was wearing long trousers so I must have been older. I set off from the same place but this time under my own steam. I tripped, simple as that. What made this descent memorable was not the curious shape I became. That was achieved with minimum fuss and maximum agony. No, this outing was distinguished by the fact I had my hands in my pockets. And I soon found you can't take your hands out of your pockets during free fall. They become clamped in. This means you can't break your fall. You are, of course, at liberty to break everything else you hold dear. The thing that impresses the passer-by during the performance is your apparent nonchalance. Even at the end, as you lie waiting for the chalk line to be drawn around you, the trousered hands lend a certain insouciance to the crime scene. You look like Burlington Bertie who rose at ten-thirty and walked down the Strand with his hat in his hand. So don't. That's my advice concerning walking downstairs with your hands in your pockets.

However, our gang did not restrict our adventures to domestic flights.

During these years, it was an economic fact that the housing market was flat, well, flattened actually. This gave birth to the concept of the adventure playground. The council didn't have to build them. They just appeared overnight, still smoking. If a house was evacuated, a big black E was painted on the front door. Who could resist that? We were in like ferrets. Of course there were wardens to protect the properties, a fine body of men. They never caught sight of us. The best playgrounds of all were houses each side of a bombed site. These were often shored up to prevent them collapsing into the crater. There was much scaffolding and planking between dwellings. The planks enabled teams of infants to carry out operations without using what was left of the stairs. Marg was once with an advance party on the fourth floor of a mansion near Onslow Square when the police arrived to secure the property. She led her platoon through a hole in the wall, across two planks, four storeys up, wheeling her doll's pram. I believe I was too young to be on this outing, though it's possible I was in the pram.

The rectangle bounded by Onslow Square, Fulham Road, Selwood Terrace and Brompton Road was our patch. It was far enough from home to count as being away, yet it was within easy reach. It was largely deserted. There were plenty of big Es. The houses had fine rooms, high ceilings, some open to the skies. There were spooky cellars and grand staircases to slide down. What more could a boy want? A banana, that's what. At this stage of my life I'd never seen a banana. That aside, I still warm to London SW7. Sometimes, if the raking light of evening catches a front door at just the right angle, I fancy I can still see an odd E, pentimento beneath the gloss.

Chapter XVI
The felt collar.

Long before the invention of estate agents, Chelsea Creek was charmingly called Chelsea Creek. Long before the invention of supermarket trolleys the citizens had nothing to throw in the creek except prams, bicycle wheels, body parts and any other landfill they cared to lob over the parapet of the King's Road bridge. The railway, our railway, ran below the bridge. The Creek didn't quite make it. It followed the rails until it reached the bridge and there it stopped. There it curdled and festered in a sludge, as fine a body of slime as you could wish for. Fetid air hung above it like a shroud. Disease and lamentation cankered its dank heart. It soiled itself with the mulch of its own decomposition.

It was magnetic. And probably radioactive.

It was also hard to reach. Once there, and this was part of its appeal to a right-minded child, you couldn't get back. It should have been called the Chelsea Bourn. It was the undiscovered country from which no traveller returns, at least, not the way they came. The creek was rarely wet. The river tides were fitful. If a swollen one fingered its dubious way into this backwater, the creek was not cleansed. The probing waters merely disturbed the turbid debris. The layers of putrefaction shifted and twitched, as if alive, but near death. The creek didn't splosh, it 'spolshed'. It wheezed emphysematic heaves and gave off putrid airs. All was mucous in the state of stagnant.

Here's how to get there.

There were two routes. Well, three really, but the third involved dying en route so we'll skip those directions. Actually, there were four ways, if you include the swan's way. Now and then some oil-soaked waterfowl or a bewildered swan might paddle up the creek by mistake and be brought to a halt by the increasing viscosity. They'd look around moodily, then fly away, usually honking. The easy route was over the fence by the station, skulk along the platform, under the King's Road bridge - and under the watchful eye of the signal box - turn left up the bank and drop down into the mire. The other way was to risk a quick dash from the cut by the Nell Gwynne called Rewell Street. This was an unmade road back then. From the pub, the street sloped down past the timber yard and led to the gasworks. On the left ran a high wooden fence. Beyond that lay the forbidden world; the overgrown embankment, the railway lines, then more banking and finally the creek. If you were brave, you climbed the fence and made a dash for it. The peril in this route was because the signal box stood in your path. You could see the box if you climbed the lamppost by the fence, half way down the cut. From there you could case the joint. I was perched at the top of the lamppost one day, sitting astride the two cross bars, my arms clutching the glassware, when a voice from below said:

'And what might you be doing?'

It's true you know. There were definitely more policemen on the streets back then. There was a film of that era called The Blue Lamp, starring Jack Warner. Somehow, it seemed, the constable and I had entered the plot. According to him, I was tampering with a lamp on his beat. With my limbs wrapped round it, this was a difficult charge to deny. My first thought was, has the signalman seen me! The shame of it, if he has! My next worry was would the stash of counterfeit sixpences in my bedroom be found? Wormwood Scrubs loomed. A few gas workers loomed, gathering round to witness the arrest. What would happen now? A warning? A caution? No, worse than that. These were tough times. Citizens found clasping council property in close embrace, as if their life depended on it - which it would if they let go - must be dealt with firmly, hence zero tolerance of lamppost sitting.

'Name?'

'Kelso.'

'How do you spell it?

'I-t, har har!'

'You'd better watch out, lad.'

'K-e-l-s-o.'

'Address?'

'477 Fulham Road.'

'That's the pub, The Rising Sun, isn't it?'

'Yes.'

'You should know better, my lad.'

(Prisoner, to himself, 'I ain't your lad!')

The climb down was as undignified as the march home. The constable insisted on holding my shoulder as he led me away to check on my story. Holmead Road seemed a hundred miles distant. Off we went, my cheeks glowing with shame. Would Johnny or his Mum or Dad see me as we passed the Nell Gwynne? Eyes down. Never have paving stones seemed so fascinating. Turn left into King's Road, then right into Holmead. Would Billy Skinner see me? What about Charlie Riddell? The gauntlet stretched ahead. That evil chow at Number 29 went mad as we passed, snapping and lunging on its chain. It hated me, but not as much as I hated it. Every door seemed open. It's true, people did leave their doors open back then. It wasn't trust. It was to let out the smell of boiled cabbage. The perfume filled the air as the penal party passed. There's Mrs. Potts, her eyes out on stalks, cabbage stalks probably. Past Easy Audrey's - no, not her, I couldn't bear it - that would ruin my chances forever. On past Frenchy's yard. No, not him, please!

Then ringing the bell of 477.

After a long delay, and a second irritated ringing by the policeman, a bleary-eyed Uncle Reg opened the door. It was mid-afternoon, the time when Uncle Reg had his siesta. He didn't like to be disturbed. Neither would you if you were up at six every morning and never in bed until gone midnight. He wasn't one to enjoy being hassled by impatient bell-ringers at the best of times. And this wasn't the best of times to engage him in light discourse.

Jack Warner said:

'Is this yours?'

Uncle Reg woke up immediately. This was his big chance. He's-not-your-real-father-you-know looked down at he's-not-my-real-son-you-know. He's-not-my-real-son-you-know, stared at a nearby manhole cover with an intensity rarely given to his school studies. A thought was slowly dawning. Not only was I not Jack Warner's lad, I wasn't, strictly speaking, Uncle Reg's.

'What's he been up to?' said Uncle Reg.

'Up to twelve feet above a public highway in pursuance of illegal activities.'

Uncle Reg paused.

'Turn around,' he said. The one-boy identity parade turned, his eyes never leaving the ground.

'Mmm,' said Uncle Reg.

He remembered all the black wartime nights when policemen on their midnight rounds would tap on the saloon bar door and be given a nip of whisky for their trouble. Maybe he recalled the night when an unexploded incendiary bomb was found on the saloon bar step, just by the police phone box. And how he'd picked it up and carried it away to safety before warning the law. Then he'd fetched the stirrup pump and filled the water bucket for them, just in case.

'Mmm,' Uncle Reg said again. Slowly, reluctantly, there on the doorstep the stepfather in him came out.

Finally he said:

'Yes, it's one of ours.'

Severe cautions and warnings were issued.

This was not the first time I'd been brought home by the authorities. My debut, you'll remember, was on VJ night. On that occasion the family had been pleased to see me. But now my recidivism was over. I swore to never again give Uncle Reg a reason to throw me down the stairs. I hadn't enjoyed the experience the first time round, so it wasn't hard to kick the habit. The lamppost matter was never mentioned again. That was the family remedy for most things: ignore-it-therapy. It worked like a dream. The matter was never mentioned at school either. A criminal record, in those quaint days, was not yet a badge of honour in society.

Chapter XXVII
The play's the thing.

No it isn't. Not in my case. Around this time, the focus at Sloane was on the forthcoming school play, Julius Caesar. I enquired as to what form Julius was studying in but didn't get a reply. What I did get was a summons to the Headmaster's study to audition for a part. The Head's study was where boys were taken to be punished, caned. This added a frisson of theatrical excitement to the venue. I should explain I disliked any kind of public appearance. My dislike partly stemmed from my performances of 'There's a cupboard under the stairs' with Charlie Harris in the audience. Public speaking and the spotlight were not for me. Stage fright had come upon me early. Mum said she could remember when I was a baby walking me in my pram and, even then, I'd insist on a towel - a safety curtain - being hung in front of the hood so I couldn't see out and no one could see in. Mind you, we were on holiday in Clacton at the time, so this may have been the early onset of discernment.

Auditions were held in front of the Headmaster, Guy Boas, and one other gent, the School Secretary, a lanky sort of beak whose name escapes me. There was no sign of Julius Caesar. Maybe they wanted me for the lead? I stood before the Headmaster's imposing desk and was handed the text and invited to read the bit about lending your ears to somebody. I was three lines in and going strongly when the School Secretary said pointedly:

'Aloud!'

'Out loud,' added the Headmaster.

Embarrassing! But they should have said!

Considering my nerves, the interruption didn't faze me. I set off confidently once more. If you have experience of the boards, you'll know the great advantage of reading a part is you don't have remember the words. However, there is one thing you must remember, and after a while it seemed I hadn't. I don't know how many near-death experiences you've had. In my case, mercifully few, but those crises I have endured shared one thing in common. To begin with, your hearing goes. Now, as I read on, I was listening carefully to myself declaiming about Caesar's ambition and how it was a grievous fault. That's when a grievous fault came over my ears. At first I wondered if the person I'd lent them to a few lines earlier, had failed to give them back. I could barely hear a thing. Then, faintly, I heard voices.

School Secretary: 'He's sounding faint.

Headmaster: 'He's looking faint.'

School Secretary: 'He has forgotten to breathe.'

Headmaster: 'It is a grievous fault.'

School Secretary: 'Shall I remind him, O Caesar?'

Headmaster: 'Catch him first. The rest of him is joining in the faint.'

School Secretary: 'Breathe, boy.'

Still silently mouthing the timeless verse, Marcus Antonius was caught and half-dragged outside, his heels drumming a light tattoo on the parquet. They sat him on a wooden chair and the School Secretary's secretary, Portia, brought him a glass of water. Very refreshing, water at certain times. His hearing returned and with it came voices from the study.

School Secretary: 'Spear carrier?'

Headmaster: 'We'll never get insurance.'

School Secretary: 'Front of house?'

Headmaster: 'If he can find it.'

The failed auditionee exited left, through the swing doors, passing the next victim on his way in.

'How did it go? said the newcomer.

'Swimmingly,' I said.

That's the trouble with Shakespeare for me, swimming. The words, the images, make my head swim. I lose the narrative because, as each new phrase changes - 'place with that which goes before, in sequent toil' - the beauty breaks my concentration. I want to repeat the phrases, to hear them over and over again like music. Of course, I didn't feel like that then. Shakespeare had yet to work his spell. I couldn't know a lifetime later I'd be left just as speechless.

So, the world of the theatre was not for me.

Neither was the world of Mr. Nightingale, our maths teacher. He was a tall man with a long neck and a prominent Adam's apple. This fascinated me. My head would nod up and down in time with its movement. He took this nodding as a sign I understood his teaching. Wrong. The only thing I retained about mathematics was the nodding. To this day, I nod as if in agreement even while lamenting in disbelief over say, my bank statement.

Let's be clear about this.

It wasn't that I was disinterested in schooling, or more than usually idle. Indeed, I was keen, even eager at times. I took it all in, it just didn't stick. I've heard it said memory is intelligence, or was it the other way round? Of course, some information was retained. Yet in the main, my recall was rather like that other expression of memory, the one that enables some materials - plastics and metals for example - to return to their original shape after being deformed. I took facts on board for a while, but then my mind would gradually return to its original empty shape. I'd also developed by this time, a mild case of ask-me-a-question-itis. Under certain circumstances, the moment I'm questioned about something, even something I know well, the answer goes out of my head. I've never been able to isolate the circumstances under which the information either goes or stays. Maybe I was experiencing senior moments when I was a junior.

Mind you, not everything is forgotten, more's the pity.

'Lars Porsena of Clusium
By the Nine Gods he swore
That the great house of Tarquin
Should suffer wrong no more.
By the Nine Gods he swore it,
And named a trysting day,
And bade his messengers ride forth,
East and west and south and north,
To summon his array.'

I've carried Lord Macaulay's, Lars Porsena, around unwanted in my head for years. And the last lines still sound as bad ever. 'Summon his array.' I ask you. The trouble is, I know thousands of snippets like this. Take 'merulius lachrymans'. This, I think, is dry rot. A carpenter half a century ago said the words to me. Why should I never forget them? As for the 1814 Congress of Vienna, don't get me started on that, or Garibaldi and the unification of Italy. I have random facts stuck to me like those little yellow stickers with nothing cohesive, nothing useful.

Certainly nothing useful that could be used in exams.

Exams were held in the school gymnasium with the desks set out in rows an anti-crib distance apart. We were surrounded on all sides by wooden wall bars. A master would sit at the front, invigilating. I liked the silence, the theatre of the moment. I enjoyed the sense of emptiness that came upon me. One thing I did master at Sloane was the ability to stare mindlessly into the middle distance, not meditating or daydreaming, just staring.

I don't wish to slight the teachers at Sloane School. They were as fine a body of didacts as ever wagged a finger at the youth of today. I had a good education. I just took it badly. It wasn't the teacher's fault. It wasn't even Mr. Grindal's fault, he who caned me in front of the whole class on one merciless morning, for some minor misdemeanor quite undeserving the gravity of the punishment. It certainly wasn't Mr. Allen's fault. He was a slip of a man who looked like Ghandi. He had a powerful presence. I was so frightened of him I can't even remember what subject he taught. Who else was there? Mr. Gilliland, geography, whose world was full of esparto grass. Mr. Berkeley, history, encyclopedic about Garibaldi. Mr Murphy, a bluff Pickwickian soul who taught English and was in charge of the school bookstore. This was a room, high above the snow line, in which I spent much time filing and sorting books, while inhaling dust and searching in vain for the works of Hank Janson. I enjoyed this chore although I've forgotten if it was a punishment or a privilege. And who was that Australian teacher, whose name began with M? Was he Mr. Marsden? I'm not sure but I can remember his pet hate. It was the phrase, shut up, much in vogue. He loathed it. Never a lesson went by without him telling us so. Then there was Mr. Linklater who taught French and was a good egg, being built on similar lines. He could see through people. He once explained that speaking French could be a useful way of earning money.

'Even the finest French restaurants,' he said, looking at me, 'need washers-up.'

German lessons were odd. For the first two terms, I was top of the class. But in the following term I found the language incomprehensible. How could it have become so hard in one short holiday? Latin, well, I was never offered the option. Was it a Mr. Burton who taught this? Whatever his name, he and another nameless master were reputed to speak Latin to each other for fun. There were many others, of course, in the march of the mentors. There was even one sixth-former, reputed to be a communist, who played great boogie-woogie on the school grand piano when there was no one around. He has a lot to answer for in the opinion of those to whom I would later become related. There was Mr. Ind, of physical training fame, who raised me from the dead every now and then. And there was the appropriately large, Mr. Little, who escorted school trips to Paris, France. France, where the trains ran in the streets, with no platforms or fences! You didn't have to climb lampposts to see them. You could get run over easily. Brilliant!

France introduced us to something else not found in the Fulham Road. One innocent day in Paris, the school party was taken to an outdoor swimming pool. We changed, showered and marched through the double-doors into the sunlight of the lido. There we found 30 or 40 women and girls swimming and sunbathing topless. Bushell fainted and had to be carried out on a pallet. Miller was never the same again. And I was reduced to wondering why German grammar didn't burn itself onto the retina in this memorable way.

I'm oddly interested in my schooling. I see it now as a study in ignorance. What little I've learned in life - apart from learning to read, write and drive - has been largely self-taught. What stops me learning conventionally? I was diligent, in my way. It's not that schooling is wasted on the young. Others manage to absorb and retain instruction. Is it brain capacity, sheer size? Do heads fill up like jugs? Throughout these school years, comprehension was invariably followed by the glazed look. Is there a limit to what we - as individuals - can know? I don't mean what mankind can know. I believe man will eventually know everything and 'come to know the place for the first time'. I marvel at what man has achieved. Yet one or two of us still bumble along in stone-age style. I just feel miffed that I couldn't contribute to the adventure.

Maybe Bishop was right all along. He sat next to me in 5b. We both failed our exams to get into the sixth-form. We were then told we would be sent for a year's revision to a form called Transitus. This was a holding bay between the fifth and sixth years.

'Transitus,' I said. 'What does that mean?'

'It means you're thick,' said Bishop.

Chapter XXVIII
Room at the bottom.

So Transitus it was. The little study classroom at the top of the school building, purpose built for those with a tendency to little study. Transitus was as high as I would rise in study circles. Not that I wasn't given a second chance. I was, and I was appalled. The plot was that we should all re-sit the exam. More empty hours beside the wall bars loomed. I was disappointed not because I'd failed get into the sixth form, but because I was now eligible to leave school. But the powers that be - Mum and others - had decided I should stay on for another year. Twelve months more of twopenny halfpenny football and idly punching each other in the biceps.

Were we all dunces?

Probably not. The truth is, I don't know. I've kept an eye out to see if any of my fellow scholars made a name for themselves and rose above the common herd, but no sightings so far. To my present knowledge, the current list of achievements of this happy breed is:

Fellows of the Royal Society: none.

Archbishops of Canterbury: none.

Prime Ministers: none.

Nobel prize winners: none.

Chiefs of the Imperial General Staff: none.

Doctors of Philosophy: it depends what you mean by none.

Nuclear physicists: a black hole.

Lucasian Professors of Mathematics at Cambridge University: zero.

As with the teachers, I don't wish to impugn the qualities of my fellow students. They were as fine a flock as you could ever wish to crack a conker with. They're probably all serving society in their way; forming part of that large, and largely unreported, pool of those who contribute to 'the quiet rhythm of blameless lives'. Are they all, I wonder, driving Transit vans with 'clean me' written in the grime? I doubt it. But in one way, I feel deprived. Down all my days, I've never once been able to boast, I was at school with 'him'.

Or her.

Her was Rita Tyler who lived in Callow Street near the Forum cinema. She scarred me. She burned her silhouette indelibly on my retinas without so much as a by your leave. She never knew it of course. We never met, never spoke. She was older than me and vastly more curved. She went to Carlyle School for Girls. She certainly qualified as a girl. I was in no doubt of that. One glance that's all it took, one afternoon on my way to the pictures, right there on Fulham Road. She was standing on the other side of the thoroughfare, just past the Belisha beacon. I was marked, never to fully recover.

Girls shouldn't be allowed to do that.

The exam we were studying for - or as Mr. Murphy would say - 'the examination for which we were studying' has been reissued in many cover versions and given many different titles in the ensuing decades. What was it then? Matriculation, School Certificate, General Certificate of Education? No idea. All I can recall is that you had to pass in five subjects to have 'passed'. If you didn't pass in five subjects you hadn't 'passed' even if you had passed some of the subjects. Clear? No, nor was I. But I tried hard. I set my sights on the 'easy' subjects: history, geography, English literature, English language, and art and somehow or other I scraped by and passed. While I was scraping, I was interviewed by a body called the Headmasters Employment Board.

'What do you want to do?' I was asked.

'Travel,' I lied.

I had no idea what I wanted to do. The Board said they'd oblige and did so. As a result, I spent a year boarding a Number 14 bus twice a day. It's still my favourite route, a sort of home bus. My commute was between, ding-ding, Stamford Bridge and, ding-ding, Green Park underground station, W1. The morning bus in the rush hour started from Stamford Bridge. You could always get a seat. The location is important. Fulham Road at the junction with Holmead Road and Moore Park Road widens out considerably. In the impenetrable smogs of those days - the word itself a conjunction of smoke and fog - that junction was like the Bermuda triangle for buses and drivers. They'd crawl over the railway bridge from Chelsea and were never seen again. It was a problem. And what are problems? Problems are opportunities waiting to be solved, as the yet-to-be-invented management consultants say. This opportunity led to a famous wheeze. This was the 'We'll-guide-you-through-the-fog-for-a tanner-Mister' wheeze. An enterprise set up by two local youths, one of them being Dudley's best friend.

The business plan was simple.

Where the road widened, the kerb to the left of the driver would disappear. We'd walk ahead of the bus until the driver could once more pick up the kerb of the main road in his headlights. That's how thick those smogs were. They were yellowish, you could taste them, you could very nearly eat them. They were like nothing seen since. Alas, the enterprise did not flourish. Business, like everything else about it, was slow. It was also seasonal, that too was a drawback. The other downside was the wheezing. The smogs were so bad that after an evening shift you needed a fag to clear your lungs.

So it was one morning, armed with pitiful exam results, I set off for my first job. (For tax reasons I elect to skip over the holiday jobs cleaning taxis in the garages behind Maxwell Road.) Messrs Thomas Cook & Sons, travel agents of Berkeley Street, London, W1, had the honour of being my first employer. Their offices were huge. Even the staff entrance in Stratton Street was big. The main entrance, in Berkeley Street, was spectacular. It led, down wide stone steps, into a vast pillared hall with polished wood counters on all four sides and a great square island of counters in the middle. Behind every counter were clerks, waiting to serve the traveller's every whim. There were acres of polished marble flooring, empty and bare, occupying some of the most valuable real estate in the kingdom. Before the square island stood another smaller island, a huge raised desk-cum-dais, with display brochures full of elegant ladies and gents in Panama hats cruising the Panama Canal. Behind this desk sat a quartet of uniformed hostesses receiving the passing trade with winning smiles.

'Good morning, continental travel, straight on, Sir.'

'British travel, just to your right, Madam.'

'Foreign Exchange department, to your left, Madam.'

This was traveller's banking in high style. There was none of your street corner kiosk 'change, weschel, gambio' about these exchanges.

Some months later I was a trainee on the British travel counter when a gentleman approached, his heels clicking on the marble flooring.

'I would like, please,' he said in a cultured voice, 'if my request is not too humble for these august halls, a cheap day return ticket to Battersea Park.'

Battersea Park, I should explain, is a railway station one stop out of Victoria rail terminus. From Berkeley Street it would have been quicker to walk there. The fare was sixpence. The gentleman pronounced the word 'Battersea', 'b-ter-sea'. For some reason I adopted this linguistic tic and have not been able to shake it off. Curse you, b-ter-sea Park, whoever you were.

There was much a freshman could learn in this Palladian environment.

Around this time, railway tickets were small green affairs that needed to be date stamped. The stamping machine was about the size of a coffee pot. You inserted one end of the ticket into a slot in the coffee pot and, b-boomp! the date was stamped. You then reinserted the ticket the other way around and, b-boomp! again, it was stamped at the other end. The music of this calling was singular. A skilled booking clerk, in her prime, could sound a tattoo of b-boomps that spoke of high-peak activity.

However, out of high-peak hours, idle clerks had discovered they could imitate the music by banging, first your elbow, then your wrist in rapid succession upon the counter. With two dexterous flicks of the forearm it was done: b-boomp! b-boomp! The similarity of the noise was uncanny. I soon mastered this and became adept. Whenever I was confronted with a counter - in later years this would be quite often - I would demonstrate the art. Long after the coffee pot date stamp machines and the green tickets had gone, their music consigned to the silence of history, I would continue. I have since slid from many a barstool while attempting to pass on this skill - a valuable part of our common heritage - to bemused bar staff.

There was another aspect of selling rail tickets.

In that year there was a tremendous, sickening rail crash that cost over one hundred lives. The fact of my selling rail tickets, and my innocent interest in trains, made the event seem close to home and even more horrific. In the week it happened I received a pay increase of one shilling a week. This was because, unknown to me, I was a member of the Transport Salaried Staffs Association. Joining the union was presumably a condition of employment. I had not been asked. My union dues were docked from my pay packet. I hadn't noticed. The union, the TSSA, was affiliated to ASLEF, the Associated Society of Locomotive Engineers and Fireman. Under the circumstances I couldn't help feeling, even from the dark heart of my self-centredness, the cause of the locomotive engineers and fireman was more deserving than mine.

However, before I was allowed to interface with the public on the British travel counter, I had to serve a backroom apprenticeship upstairs in Independent Travel and Transport. From the windows of the ITT department you could, if you were prepared to lean out precariously, obtain a good view of King George VI's funeral as it processed along Piccadilly.

ITT served the needs of Americans - they were nearly always Americans - who came to 'do' Europe, sometimes for weeks, sometimes for months on end. Their itineraries and ticketing had to be planned in the minutest detail. It was meticulous work: planes, trains, hotels, chauffeur driven cars, taxis, passports, permits, visas, everything had to be considered. Money was no object. These people wanted, and needed, cosseting. One mistake might leave a Texas oil baron and his brood stranded on some bleak quayside at midnight, howling for blood.

The temptation was huge.

We worked in sections of eight overseen by a team leader, in my case the fearsome Major Jimmy Theed, a veteran of the North West frontier where he had lost the sight of one eye. His good eye was the keenest gimlet that ever scanned an airline timetable or the continental Bradshaw. Its laser sharpness constantly frustrated his junior staff as they plotted to maroon the paying customers. In the course of this work, I became familiar with all the paired frontier crossings of Europe:

Cerbere/Port-Bou and a hundred others, anywhere our Texas Mr. Norris might change trains.

Oddly, along with frontier crossings, I also became familiar with the outer frontiers of opera. On my section, one of the other sirens seeking to lure travellers to their doom, was a bloke a year or two older than me called Brian. He liked opera and once a month, when funds permitted, would climb to the gods in Sadler's Wells and drink it all in. I took to joining him and uncritically soaked up the usual fare: Carmen, La Boheme, Cav and Pag, even Norma at Covent Garden with Maria Callas. Opera was preferable to queuing after work for a bus home. By the time the curtain came down, the rush hour crowds were gone and seats on the No 14 were plentiful.

During that year - it was a proscribed year as we shall see - I also saw, in Dover Street, my first art exhibition. One lunchtime, I was on my way back to my desk clutching my sandwiches and chanced upon a show by the New Yorker artist, Saul Steinberg. Waving my egg-and-tomato-on-white, I overcame my posh-gallery-shyness and went in. I wasn't a subscriber to the magazine but Saul converted me. I was hooked.

The year, then, was turning out quite good - except for King George VI, of course. But during this time, although to me it seemed as if my star was in the ascendancy, there was another elevation afoot. I was slowly rising above my station, getting too big for my boots, putting on the Ritz. This was a slow process of which I was completely unaware. It manifested itself oddly. My new sophisticated friends 'up west' seemed to occupy a worldlier world. Their ways somehow seemed superior to my homeland cellars full of light ale. My 'drum' had started to seem humdrum.

Sometimes I'd arrive home after closing time, to find the pub lights still on and Mum, Uncle Reg and perhaps one or two of the staff enjoying an after hours drink. Mum's tipple was often a small glass of Warnik's advocaat into which she would pour a drop of cherry brandy, drawing a tiny red heart upon the yellow surface. This gave the drink its name, 'bleeding heart'. She might also smoke a cigarette. Passing Clouds she preferred. They were a top brand, oval shaped. They looked like they'd been sat on. Perhaps that's why she never inhaled. She had another favourite drink, a quarter bottle of champagne. She'd drink one every morning at eleven o'clock. Despite this, Mum wasn't really a drinker or a smoker. In a way, I don't know what she was, or who she was. I'm still trying to find out.

One winter's day I was coming home from work on a No 14 bus, sitting downstairs on the front nearside seat. At the Harrods stop, I saw Mum running towards me to catch the bus. She was dressed in her best, her Canadian squirrel fur coat and fur hat. She hadn't, of course, seen me. The driver ignored her waves and smiling pleas to wait for her, and drove off without letting her get on. As we passed, she leaned towards him, gave him a gargoyle grimace and stuck her tongue out as far as a tongue can be stuck out which is a surprisingly long way if you try really hard.

He took no notice, but I did.

Who was this elegant woman, dressed to the nines, in the heart of Knightsbridge acting like an 8-year schoolgirl larking about on the Mountains of Mourne? I didn't know her, but I was impressed.

I didn't let it show.

By now, I was full of myself, full of my world, my rail tickets, my operas. They were better than the musicals Mum loved to see with an aunt or two in tow. What was Oklahoma to Verdi? In those after-hours sessions I was often dismissive and surly, rude as only someone secure in another's love, can be. For that I'm ashamed. In mitigation, you must remember I was adolescent, a teenager undergoing - as we would say today - a hormonal maelstrom. Back then it was called being a git.

Sometimes Big Pat, who had a soft spot for Mum, looked as if he'd like to disassemble me and throw away the components. Yes, it's true I worked in the pub now and then, but I was very keen to not work in the pub. On some Saturdays I'd lie in bed until all hours while downstairs and in the kitchen everyone else slaved away. No wonder somebody slung an encyclopaedia of biology at me. If ever there was a kid who needed taking down a peg, it was yours truly. Fortunately, society had at its disposal an institution designed precisely for this purpose.

It was called Her Majesty's Royal Corps of Engineers.

Chapter XXIX
Secure at last.

Never, it seems, has the nation slept easier in its bed than during my two years in the colours. The sense of security shone in people's faces. Uncle Reg and Mum appeared excessively relieved. These were trying times. The Cold War was at its height, nowhere bitterer in my experience than in Worcestershire. The Korean War was on. I had heard something about that on the news, never thinking it might have anything to do with me. This was the political climate at the time I set out from Paddington one snowy December morning to join my regiment. I left behind a London that was about to be visited by a smog that killed thousands, a smog so bad you couldn't find a bus, let alone guide one through it.

My colleagues at Thomas Cook had arranged for the guard on the train to deliver a card of best wishes and farewell to me. A cheery touch and much appreciated as I sat in the corner of the third class carriage, whimpering. I tried all the usual tricks:

head out the window in the hope of a cinder in the eye, or a friendly scalping by a passing tunnel. It wasn't to be. There was no respite.

Worcester is a fine city.

The composer Elgar had a soft spot for it I believe. He didn't dwell where I dwelt. Gerontius himself wouldn't have dreamed of dwelling where I dwelt. An army truck waited at Worcester station. Willing hands hauled me aboard. Selective, and no doubt protective, memory loss occurs here. Is 'abreaction' still practised in mental health? You remember the idea. Make patients relive their trauma in the hope it will lessen their symptoms. Make them feel the pain again. Restrain them if necessary, as they do so. Well, I'm not going to abreact my stay in that nameless camp outside Worcester. Let's just say it was, like the city, fine.

I was given a fine new set of clothes, not quite my colour, or my fit, but fine. A fine pair of boots made of iron. A fine knife, fork, spoon and mess tin. A fine bed, in a fine hut, with a fine layer of ice on its concrete floor. And a fine view of the distant, snow covered Malvern Hills, very romantic at eventide when you most felt like dying. Except you didn't only feel like dying at eventide. The feeling tended to come on with the lights, at 4.45 a.m., linger through the morning, and was not inclined to disperse through the luncheon or tea intervals. Restrain me if you will, but I'm not abreacting any more than that.

215

Except for the food.

Yes, there was food. Despite all other activities being devoted to the reduction of personal well being, food of a sort was served. Outside the exit of the mess hall was an early model dishwasher. This was a large galvanised tank filled with a stew of scalding water and bubbling grease. Into this you plunged your dirty cutlery and your lily-white hands. The bacteria clinging to your eating irons were instantly exterminated, along with your fingerprints.

Then came the cruellest cut of all. After only three weeks, just when I was getting used to having my flesh flayed, they sent me home for Christmas!

'Hello Mummy! Hello Uncle Reg! Hello Dur-Dur! I'm home. Can I wash the floors? Clean the toilets? Serve behind the bar? Sing Oklahoma? I'll do anything, for you, Mum, anything, I'll do anything for you...'

The chastened chappie with chapped hands was reformed. Homecoming! There's no love song finer, but how strange the change from minor to Sapper. No longer was I the 'street angel, house devil' as Mum had taken to calling me. And how the pub had altered in three short weeks. It was glorious. It was paradise. Who'd have thought heaven, about which I had received so much intense theological instruction, would turn up on the corner of Holmead Road? Yet there it was, Nirvana with a wines and spirit licence.

Christmas came and Christmas went.

With it went Sapper 22747462, this time to live in a hut in Guillemont Barracks, Minley Road, Cove, near Farnborough, Hampshire, the outer limits of the known world. Two years without the option. Two years at my current age takes about ten minutes. At the age I was then, two years seemed an immeasurably long time. This was partly because it was indeed a long time, but also, it now seems such an immeasurably long time ago. It is as if all this took place not long after the Big Bang. Perhaps I should have brought back samples of the atmosphere and a few rocks. If I had, scientists wouldn't have needed to build the large hadron collider to find out how the world began. As it was, unknown to me, I was about to collide with Regimental Sergeant Major Taylor R.E.

Me, an engineer! It was the birth of irony.

Army uniforms were made of coarse material. They were uncomfortable, they didn't fit, and they abraded. As you marched, you trailed behind you a fine dust of your own skin cells. The costume was topped off with a beret, very French, very painterly. The new recruit - the sprog - could be easily spotted by the bagginess of his beret. The beret of the old hand, the soldier who had 'got some time in', who had 'got his knees brown', wasn't baggy. It was small, tight, neat, very hard man. But how to reduce the bagginess? The safe way is by repeated rinsing and drying of the cloth portion - never the leather rim.

This takes time. Unfortunately among us was Mr. Shortcut, a regular soldier - he hadn't been press-ganged - who worked in the kitchens. He said, for a consideration, he'd help. Innocently, we offered up our headwear. Overnight the berets were placed in a warming oven. They returned in reduced circumstances, rims and all. They wouldn't fit our heads. Someone had a grapefruit and one by one we tried our hats on it. Mine fitted perfectly, lending the fruit an enviable, veteran squaddy look.

Our parade the following morning struck no fear into the hearts of the distant North Korean armies. Military legal proceedings followed. So, hats off to the catering corps. We took little comfort from the fact that the oaf had shrunk his own hat. Plans were afoot to boil his head to make it fit.

What the European Court of Human Rights didn't know, partly because it hadn't yet been formed, was that basic training in the British army was 8 weeks, but in the Royal Engineers it was 16 weeks. Four months of square bashing!

Enter RSM Taylor, RE.

If ever there was a man with whom you did not want to mess it was he. I had definitely never seen him, or his kind, in the gods at Sadler's Wells. He was all my authority figures rolled into one: the nuns, the priests, Mum, Uncle Ed, Guy Boas, not forgetting Uncle Reg in one of his throw-me-down-the-stairs moods. The RSM marched everywhere gripping a mechanical pace stick, giant dividers that paced out invisible paths of glory. He was the most respected man in Christendom and all the other doms. He emanated power, authority and gravity. When he passed by, platoons of recruits, civilians, vehicles even, would freeze. The waves would part. The earth would open. Subduction occurred in the region. Have you ever tried typing while standing to attention? I'm doing so now. That was RSM Taylor.

Fortunately, square bashing was regularly interrupted in order for us to join in other Guillemont training activities, each lasting a gruelling week.

There was basic bridging.

The principles of this were simple. Find a piece of hard ground. Then find another piece of hard ground. Then join them together with timber and rope. The venue for this pastime was the flattest piece of Hampshire known to man. For years, this featureless expanse of iron hard open ground was bridged over every fortnight by a new intake of recruits. Each resulting bridge was 30 metres long, a lorry's width wide, and stood ten centimetres off the ground. This allowed all shipping less than ten centimetres in height, safe passage below without let or hindrance.

Then came 'plastic explosives for all' week.

During this instruction I learned the curious fact that, simply touching some of these explosives with your bare hands, could induce violent headaches. The plastics came in sticks like plasticine and smelled of marzipan. They put me off fruitcake for years. Do you remember that old movie about the River Kwai? Where the prisoners built a wooden railway bridge? Then bang! It blew up. Then crash! It fell down. Cove was like that on alternate Thursdays.

There were other subjects too.

Basic knots and lashings. That could have been useful information for later life. But I didn't take it in. All I could think of was the cartoon drawing of the ravished girl on the yacht, saying:

'He told me there was a storm coming up and, like a fool, I let him tie me to the mast.'

The specialité de la maison Guillemont was Bailey bridging.

We were taught this skill during what was called hernia week. Switch your mind, if you will, to Meccano mode. Once upon time there was a man called Sir Donald Bailey who hit on an idea for rupturing all future generations of enlisted men. It worked wonderfully throughout wartime Europe and continues to this day all over the world including India. Ghandi, by the look of him, may well have had a go at Bailey bridging in his youth.

This, in essence, is how Bailey bridging works.

You took a Bailey panel, an immensely heavy, rectangular diamond-braced frame of iron girders, and stood it against another Bailey panel so they formed a pair. You then passed three pick axe handles through the panels, front, back and centre. Six Sappers, three each side, cradled the handles in the crook of their elbows. On the command, one, two, three lift, quick march, the team would totter off in an uncontrollable meander. Progress was slow. If at the outset, all six Sappers weren't facing the same way - which often happened - progress wouldn't even begin. It was hazardous work. The panels were tied together with Bailey pins. These were immense iron bolts that were sledge hammered through aligned holes in the panels. If the ear of one of the six Sappers was too close to the hole when the pin came through - which also often happened - then there were five you might say.

Have you ever done that party trick where you lean and press your arm against a wall for a few moments, then stand clear and your arm involuntarily rises? Well, after carrying a double Bailey panel around for a while, it was not unusual to see six soldiers levitate as one to a good altitude. The Bailey entertainment didn't stop there. Having got together one six-man team, with their immense burden, the regiment then found another team complete with their panel. The teams stood alongside each other, panting and clutching their groins, while other worker ants fixed roadway transoms between the two panels. The front end of the resulting U-shaped contraption was then manhandled onto a convenient tree trunk that would act as a roller. Meanwhile, two other teams would attach a duplicate contraption to the rear end. Thus the bridge grew. The whole Meccano outfit was then rolled forward, inch by sinew-cracking inch, out over a local chasm, Doom Hollow.

There was some joy to be had here.

To encourage the workforce, as you inched forward, an NCO - the Bridge Master with his neat hard man beret - would stand precariously on a topmost girder and bellow words of the Yo-oh-heave-Ho variety as he and the bridge were carried higher and higher out over the canyon. One wobble and he would be a goner. How we tried, how we shimmied, how we shook, all to no avail. We never so much as induced a tremor in the iron. We tried for a week to kill the Bridge Master in public but we couldn't dislodge him.

Compared to this, square bashing was easy.

Of course these joys couldn't last. The four months passed and we 'passed out'. Where would we be posted? Eagerly we awaited the news being pinned on to the regimental notice board. There were only three recruits with surnames beginning with K. In alphabetical order, I was in the middle. The one above me was posted on active service to Korea. The one below was posted to the British Embassy in Washington, U.S.A! Washington! Envy ran through the ranks. Even RSM Taylor looked green about the gills.

As for 22747462, where would he finish up?

Chapter XXX
Korea? Washington? Cove!

Cove, that's where 22747462 finished up. He was posted within the regiment to become a Lance Corporal, weapons training instructor. I should have told you that during basic training, while on a 48-hour pass, I told Mum I had been invited to go before an officer selection board.

'Oh,' said Mum. 'You don't want to rise above your station.'

My station at the time was Walham Green, since renamed Fulham Broadway. On my return to the regiment, I reported Mum's decision to my Officer Commanding. He listened and, while still looking at me, called for the next interviewee to enter by bellowing out what I presume was the man's name:

'Pratt!'

The army had an assortment of weapons. There was the Lee Enfield .303 rifle, a cross between a musket and a Kalashnikov. Its instruction manual read: 1. Point. 2. Shoot. Then there was the Bren gun, the 'finest light machine gun ever made'. Its instructions read: 1. Point. 2. Shoot. 3. Continue shooting until war ends. (Odd name, Bren; it's a contraction of Brno and Enfield brought about because the design was based on a Czech machine gun and it was made in Enfield.) Then there was the Sten gun, justly famous for its jams. Instructions: 1. Point. 2. Shoot. 3. Run. Finally, the .38 Webley revolver, known to me from my top-of-the-wardrobe days. This was similar to the pistols used in cowboy films. In national service hands the revolver kicked wildly. Its manual read: 1. Point. 2. Shoot. 3. Surrender.

I was assigned to a small team that worked in the weapons store, next door to the regimental armoury, near the 25-yard shooting range. This was the personal fiefdom of Quarter Master-Sergeant Gerald Fitzgerald, a respected and admired NCO. He was, as far as anyone can be in military uniform, cool. A superb shot with all weapons, he'd 'got some in', having been a prisoner of the Japanese, an experience about which he never spoke. He was tall, rangy and wore the ultimate hard man beret. With a poncho and a cigar, he could have been Clint Eastwood. Being rangy came in handy as we spent most of our time on Ash Ranges, a nearby blasted heath. Week after week herds of recruits, harried by instructors, humped ammunition boxes back and forth between the 100, 200, 300 and 500 yard firing points. From these, they would pour lead into the distant

224

butts, occasionally hitting one of the heavy metal plate targets as they did so. There were, of course, no such things as ear defenders. The noise did nothing for your hearing.

Ears came into the picture in another way on one occasion. At the end of each day the range had to be cleared of litter. The empty ammunition cartons were collected and burnt with other paper rubbish.

It was inevitable, come to think of it.

One day one of the cartons wasn't empty. It contained a lonely .303 bullet. The box was thrown on the fire. When it exploded the bullet shot out and clipped the ear lobe of a suitably startled recruit. Ear lobes can bleed profusely. They're also difficult to bandage, especially for trainee military doctors. When the wounded man appeared in the evening mess hall, he did not go unnoticed. Did you ever see the film, The Legend of the Mummy? Two eyeholes and a cake hole, I swear, and the rest of him shrouded in mystery.

Ash Ranges held another allure. The ranges were on high ground that overlooked, in the distance, the Royal Aircraft Establishment at Farnborough. This was the golden age of jet fighter development. Neville Duke and other famous test pilots regularly blasted the marksmen on the ranges out of their bunkers.

'Here comes Red leader, he's coming in now, over the black sheds, buffeting, buffeting...'

We had a grandstand view of all the prototypes: the Hunter, the Lightning, the DH 111, the Swing Wing. Saw them! We had to duck to avoid them. For me, they were the new trains. This was the show of shows. By the time of the annual Farnborough Air Show, we'd seen it all. That was one reason I gave it a miss the year of the tragic crash that killed so many spectators. The good thing about Cove was it was near home. The downside was it was a training regiment. There was a great deal of square bashing to be enjoyed along with the regular blast of passing jet planes.

Funny word, cadre, isn't it. I'd never heard of it until I was sent on one. Cadre: 'the nucleus of trained professional servicemen forming the basis for the training of new units or other military expansion', says my dictionary. It was what we might now call a training course - or a war crime. It didn't half hurt, Mum.

The Royal Corps of Engineers were parsimonious with travel warrants. When I learned I was to be sent on a cadre, I innocently asked:

'Where to?'

To a hut on the other side of the square, I was told.

'Not Korea? Not Washington?'

Learning RSM Taylor would take the cadre didn't enhance the lack of travel prospects. In a way, the course was a backward step. During the 16 weeks of basic training, beds played a big part in our lives. Not that we were in them much. But we had to build wooden box frames and place them under our blankets so the beds were neat and squared off during the day. At night, we stood the frames against the wall while we blanco'd our webbing, spat and polished our boots, and briefly slept. The cadre was like basic training over again. It was out with the hammer and nails and make more bed frames.

The aim of the cadre seemed to be to replace our spines with ramrods. To this day, if I lie flat on my back, the only parts of me that touch the floor are my heels and the back of my head.

'Shortest on the left, tallest on the right, in three ranks, size! You had a good home when you left, right, left, right!'

We quick marched, we slow marched, we drilled, we stamped the barrack square flat. We sloped arms. We presented arms. We eyes righted, we eyes lefted, we eyes fronted, and we halted with thunderous stamps that registered on the Richter scale. The bore of my rifle barrel shone like the Kohinoor diamond. My coarse gauge sandpaper battle dress was ironed and pressed to the texture of finest cashmere. The toecaps of my pig iron boots reflected light better than the Hubble telescope. Our whole beings, our very body plans were re-wrought to the perpendicular. All upright things, telegraph poles and the like, hung their heads in shame as we passed.

Overseeing all this was the RSM. Scrupulously fair, he was like Major Jimmy Theed with an added gimlet. His word was law. He was the law. And he taught military law in one unforgettable 40-minute lesson. He stood at the blackboard one morning, in front of the class as we sat taking notes. With him on the platform sat a stern faced military police corporal.

A Sapper at the back of the class asked a question. The RSM's answer didn't seem to satisfy him and he argued, talking back disrespectfully.

'What was that?' growled the RSM.

The class quivered with tension. The man lost his temper and stood up, his chair loudly scraping the floor. He shouted:

'You can keep your effing law and your effing marching you stupid c-u-...!'

'Class! Attention!' roared RSM Taylor.

As one the class sat bolt upright, quaking with fear.

'Corporal, arrest that man!'

The military policeman raced forward and seized the culprit.

RSM Taylor pointed:

'You, in the front row. What did that man say?'

'Sir,' came the reply, 'he...he said you were a b-b-bloody fool and ... and....'

The RSM turned. 'You,' he pointed, 'you in the third row. What exactly did that man say?

'Sir, sir, he said, 'eff…eff… he, he didn't like eff…'

One by one the RSM interrogated the class. Everyone had a different recollection. None of us knew exactly what had been said. We were all too scared by the drama of the moment. That, of course, was the point of the lesson. Eyewitnesses are fallible.

The lesson struck home. Even those who had fainted remembered it clearly. The argumentative Sapper was, of course, a plant. He was a member of the regimental police. They enjoyed this chore hugely.

Like all pleasures, the cadre eventually came to an end. I was elevated to full corporal. This meant a pay rise. I can't say how much it was, but bear in mind the electron microscope was in its infancy.

Promotion was good. Many Sappers I knew had sought promotion by trying to transfer to the Royal Army Educational Corps. This was thought of as a skive. The minimum rank was Sergeant, with pay to match, and the work seemed to be mostly mooching about indoors wearing shoes. The downside was, being a sergeant, every now and then you were required to be parachuted into Aldershot on a Saturday night to help the Military Police sort out your brothers-in-arms, who'd popped into town for a quick rape and pillage.

Promotion meant I was now given a room of my own, in charge of a hut whose occupants were mostly Physical

Education instructors. They were large, muscular, and I took care to give them no trouble. They wore horizontally striped jerseys in red and black. When not educating physically, they spent most of their time outdoors, often upside down on the peaked roof of the hut, walking about on their hands. It wasn't showing off, it's just what you do if you're a PE instructor off duty.

There was one result of the cadre that was less welcome and was definitely not for the squeamish. All that stamping about on the parade ground could cause bodily harm. There is an old and coarse army joke: 'What are haemorrhoids?' Answer: 'Haemorrhoids are piles for the h'arseholes of the h'aristocracy.' I didn't say it was funny. There was little about this subject that raised a smile in my quarters, especially my hindquarters. I had thought the shot ear lobe had bled a lot, but it was as nothing.

An iron rule in the army is never report sick in a training regiment. This is because the medics are far more inexperienced than you. The risks were uninsurable. The doctor on duty when I reported looked like he came from a good background and was facing a bad foreground. I could tell he'd failed many an autopsy in his time. I reported my symptoms. He could hardly bear to look and who could blame him?

'Excused boots, lie down till it gets better.'

An army bed, at heart, is an iron frame covered with chicken wire. On top of the wire are placed three thin, square shaped mattresses, called biscuits. Army fire precautions at that time consisted of a red bucket filled with sand, one per billet.

Haemorrhoids treatment, palliative, Sappers, for the use of:

1. Remove sand from fire bucket. 2. Place bucket below bed. 3. Remove middle biscuit. 4. Lie down on back, facing ceiling. 5. Bleed. 6. Empty bucket as necessary. 7. Repeat. 8. When recovered, rinse bucket, replace sand.

This treatment can be draining. And there was no privacy. I overheard two squaddies from the motor pool as they passed my window.

'Seen Kelso lately?'

'I think he's gone for a bleed.'

I felt like a brake system.

So, rule one, never report sick in a training regiment; rule two, on pain of lingering death, never ever go to a military hospital. But I had no choice. It wasn't that I was losing too much blood. It was because we were running out of buckets. I was sent to Cambridge Military Hospital, Aldershot. To be fair - and by now I was pale white - the staff here were not inexperienced. The team assigned to me were just back from Rorke's Drift. The hospital famously incorporated many of Florence Nightingale's ideas after the Crimean War. By the feel of what was going on behind me, they were still using her lamp to conduct investigations.

My condition was not uncommon in the army and treatment was well rehearsed.

The male nurse scraped rust from a batch of hypodermic needles. The doctor put down his book, The Grapes of Wrath, I couldn't help noticing. They then took turns to throw the hypodermics, assegai fashion, at the exposed area, aiming for veins. Every time they threw, a cry went up from the patient. Every time they hit a vein, a cry went up from the medics: '180!'

Until I was recruited, I had imagined if you were in the army, the thing you'd be most frightened of was the enemy. Stupid boy!

Rhododendrons, too, played their part in my military medical history. I wish they hadn't. The cool-climate evergreen rhododendrons - sometimes called the Asiatics - with their colourful blooms, can be found in the Himalayas, southwestern China and northern Myanmar, but others are scattered across northern Asia, Europe, North America and outside the Sergeant's Mess in Minley Road, Cove.

This adventure, you see, was a matter of hospitality. Or to put it differently, it was a way of putting the word hospital, into hospitality. The fact was, as time went by, even though discipline in the regiment remained iron hard, things relaxed somewhat. The regular soldiers would eventually show reluctant acceptance of the national servicemen. This was unfortunate because the regulars were at their most dangerous when friendly. On one fateful occasion an invitation was issued to several corporals to take evening drinks in the Sergeant's Mess. This was an honour. It nearly finished up with full military honours.

The hand that extended the invitation belonged to a Scots sergeant whose name I shall not disclose. It's not that I have forgotten it, oh no, it's etched on my liver. He was a short man, standing about three kilts high. He had an unexploded air about him. The carouse went well. The evening went well. The night set in. Casualties were removed at regular intervals. The iron gang, the brave last half dozen, would play one final round of Jock's Wee Game. This was a form of race, with little connection to the human race. Fresh supplies of rhododendrons were fetched from the shrubbery and laid, one flower and a leaf or two, like a buttonhole spray, on the floor on the far side of the Mess. The floor was awash with what had once been fine ale, fag ends and mulched potato crisps. The six stood facing the bar, a pint of bitter before them, with a double whisky chaser by its side.

On Jock's command, 'Go!' the pint must be downed in one. You then crawled on hands and knees across the floor, picked up your flower, ate it, crawled back to the bar, sank the chaser, about turned, stood to attention and shouted:

'Present and correct, Sir'.

The first to do this was the winner. There were no winners, this being the tenth heat of the evening. In Mandalay, 'the dawn came up like thunder'. That was nothing to what came up in Minley Road.

Rhododendron plants enjoy a freely draining, acidic soil with a pH level between 4.5 and 5.5. You may improve soils by adding organic matter such as compost or stomach contents.

'Full many a glorious morning' nearly became full many a glorious mourning. If this was what went on in the Sergeant's Mess, what on earth must it be like in the Officer's Mess? I came to the conclusion Mum had been right. I couldn't have taken much more hospitality.

Exactly two years to the day, reeking of cordite, I handed in my cap badge.

Chapter XXXI
Peace breaks out.

I let a decade or two slip by then one day, on a whim - well, actually on a bus - I returned for a nostalgic look at my old army hut. It wasn't there. Neither were the rhododendrons. Nor the Sergeant's Mess, the barrack square, or any sign of the whole camp. I couldn't even find where it had been. There was no trace of my fire bucket. It was as if the earth had moved. In fact, the earth had moved. A motorway had shown up nearby and the whole of the regimental edifice had disappeared like a wraith.

It probably hasn't gone far, or so I like to think. Those Bailey panels would slow them down. The phantom lads are probably still tottering along trying to shake off some ghostly Bridge Master.

So there I was, demobbed. As the song says: 'Free again, I'm free, to be again, to be...'

The first thing I did was to buy a green suit from Meakers, gents outfitters, of Hammersmith. In certain lights it shone slightly. I knocked on Thomas Cook's door, but my old boss had left to join a travel agency in the City. I teamed up with him for a while. Then sister Margaret called. She said a friend of a friend of hers, who ran a commercial art studio, was looking for someone to put clean water in the artist's water pots. The water they were using was so dirty their artwork was turning muddy.

Commercial artwork in those days was still done by hand, using paints and brushes. 'There is a tide in the affairs of men' and mine was of muddy water. The art college of life was calling. I changed the water pots. I made the tea. The artists said they couldn't tell the difference. I ran messages. I fetched sandwiches. I clerked. I entered the artist's time sheets on the back of job sheets, ready for invoicing. The time sheets were my introduction to the creative side of advertising. They were supreme examples of man's imagination. I delivered finished jobs to clients. And largely, I think, because of my green suit I was occasionally sent to collect a brief.

Let me tell you what the company did. I don't expect you to believe me but at the risk, in these days of revisionist history, of using the dreaded T-word I promise this is the truth. The business was not listed on the Stock Exchange. I think it had only recently been connected to the telephone exchange. It was a loose-knit 12-man band, as motley a collection of rent-a-desk freelancers as ever drew fairy tales on a time sheet. The main clients of the enterprise were mail order catalogues. These were mostly in the north, some in Manchester and one in Worcester, of unkind memory. They farmed out huge amounts of artwork to studios in London. We were known as a specialist shoe studio. We drew shoes. Honest! You see, incredibly, in this era it was thought shoes could not be photographed. Don't ask me why! Go back and look at the ads of the time. Every pair of shoes you see is an airbrushed drawing. Even more bizarre, the shoe drawings were produced on the assembly line principle.

To begin with I'd drive north and collect a bootful of shoes. These were handed to the first man on the line, the tracer-down. He had, on a spike, an outline tracing of every shoe fashion since mankind stopped wearing sealskins. He'd stub out his hand-rolled fag, hold a shoe up to the light, squint at it with an expert eye, and announce:

'Ladies, court, medium heel, square section, pointy toe.'

He'd then rummage through his tracings until he found something like it. For all I know, this may be how Manolo Blahnik works today, though I suspect not. The tracer would draw a new outline, based on the old tracing but with suitable changes, and transfer it to the art board. He'd then pass shoe and board to the airbrush man. This magician would mask off the area and airbrush all the subtleties of shape, curve and colour that the photographer's art was thought incapable of capturing. Then artwork and shoe were passed to the welter. He did nothing but draw welts and stitches. The eyelet and laces man followed the welter. There was even a broguer who did nothing but holes. I said you wouldn't believe me.

Shoe drawings were not the atelier's only stock in trade. Other illustrations were produced. These included many fine scenes of war, conflict, death and destruction for use as packaging on model aircraft kit boxes. These were done in the style I'd tried to imitate in my bit-of-bush days. The company was also a photographic retouching studio, working for ad agencies and direct clients all over London. I should point out the photographic retouching you now achieve so easily on computer was once a laborious and skilled handcraft. These skills were expensive and were charged for by the hour, minute by minute, as noted on the scrupulous time sheets. Working with these noble artisans gave me a good grounding in art appreciation.

One day a large and complex illustration had been completed. It had taken weeks to do and bore a four-figure price tag. It was so important the client came to us to collect it. One by one the protective cover papers were lifted to reveal the masterpiece. The client scanned it with his eagle eye, then said:

'Will it fit in my bag?'

We were reminded of Rembrandt's patron who cut off a slice of the 'Night Watch' canvas to get it through a door.

Another lost art practised by the workforce, was lettering. Headlines and other display words were often hand drawn and a skilled craft it was. Just like the shoe man's spike of outlines, any letterer worth his salt had a pile of tracings of those staple words of the advertiser's art: Free! New! and Sale! These words were always complete with their excitable exclamation marks. Letterers also worked on what were called 'mechanicals' or 'paste-ups' the backbone of the commercial art world. Paste-ups were the artwork that you now do on screen using Quark or InDesign or similar software. The business prospered and the work was hard. I pounded the pavements day and night carrying my artwork bag.

'At least it keeps you off the streets,' Mum said.

Mail order catalogues were not our only clients.

A major toy company also featured in the sales ledger. The marketing director, who briefed the work to me was, I found out, the co-owner of the studio I worked for! He was the partner of my Managing Director. Strange! What a coincidence! What were the chances of that happening, I thought? Or was I learning a lesson in business I didn't know I was being taught?

One day, one of our clients, an international ad agency, invited our studio manager and me to join forces and set up a studio within the agency. Two years later, having lost their major account, the agency invited us 'to take a walk till your hat floats,' as Uncle Reg liked to say. Having been poached, we were scrambled.

From the heights, we took up residence in a basement off Berkeley Square, joining an existing and ailing photographic studio. The studio manager soon tired of life below stairs and left to open a grocer's shop in the western marches. Grocery's gain was retouching's loss. Alone, and in a further attempt to market my limited ability, I made myself into a limited company and never again worked as an employee for anyone. Another tragic error of judgement.

They say, of course, in life it's not what you know, but whom you know. This filled my world with opportunity. I knew nothing and nobody. Until, at a party one evening, I found myself talking to the man who altered my course forever.

Jack McCarthy, sculptor, artist, teacher and inspiration to anyone fortunate enough to meet him. He and his wife Molly, then working as a model for the top London fashion house, Hardy Amies, became lifelong friends. If ever a man's story deserves be told, it is Jack's. No thumbnail sketch does him justice.

At the outbreak of war he volunteered, aged 17, to join the Royal Navy. After basic training he served on the destroyer, HMS Icarus, on escort duties with the Russian convoys in winter. He was commissioned as a midshipman and then served on an American built frigate on North Atlantic convoys. Shortly before D-Day, he was transferred to the staff of NOIC Isle of Wight for the period of the invasion. He was Officer in Charge of Nab Tower and was involved in the rescue of the crew of HMS Wrestler, which had struck a mine off Juno beachhead. After VE day, he was sent to the German submarine base at Kiel. He was Duty Officer on a captured German cruiser. Each morning, a high-ranking German officer, with his entourage of officers, would report to him for ship's rounds, the daily morning inspection. Ashore, the meagre RN pay was worth a fortune. Hard currency could buy whatever you wanted, food, drink, cigarettes. One cigarette could buy a woman. Jack was 21 years old. He left the navy and returned to the bank. They, grudgingly, gave him his job back. He worked as a remittance clerk for one morning. Then, finishing listing a pile of cheques, he slipped a paper band around them and wrote on it, in large letters, Goodbye! And he walked out. He went to Art College and became a successful sculptor and designer rising to the very top of his profession. Had I known his story, which I gradually gleaned over time, I would have been inhibited about talking to him so openly. Instead I told him I was interested in art and keen to learn.

'Well, come round to the studio to see us on Sunday,' he said.

I point out this detail as a caution to any of today's sculptors who may make free with their invitations. I turned up on

Jack and Moll's doorstep every Sunday for many years. Jack's was one of a row of artists' studios in Sydney Mews, South Kensington.

His next-door neighbours were, on one side Sandra Blow, R.A. and on the other, Henry Carr, R.A., both fine painters. That first visit was a revelation. I showed Jack the small portfolio of drawings I'd made down the years, many of them cartoons done while in the army. He was encouraging far beyond their merit. I said I wanted to learn to paint.

'Have a go,' he said. 'You can borrow my brushes and paints.'

'What shall I paint?' I asked.

'One subject is as good as another,' he said.

We set up an easel outside in the mews and I began to paint the scene at the far end. A brick wall closed off the cul-de-sac and beyond that was the back of one of those handsome houses in which I'd played during their evacuated years. After a while, I came to a halt.

'The wall I've painted looks nothing like the real wall,' I said.

Jack and looked at the painting, then at the wall.

'That's because your wall has a different number of rows of bricks,' he said.

'But from here I can't see how many rows the real wall has,' I said.

He looked at me tolerantly and, with the courtesy that no doubt impressed the high-ranking German officer on that captured cruiser, said:

'Then go and count them!'

That's what I have been doing ever since, counting the bricks.

This lesson in opening your eyes acted as a counterweight to those occasions in Sydney Mews when we all had to shut our eyes. This was because of Buster. Jack and Moll, you see, did not live alone. They had a pet. Pet! You should have seen it! Buster was the most massive boxer dog the world has known. He was bigger than any human boxer. He was immense and immensely affectionate to all, even his enemies, whom he destroyed by bowling them over and licking them to death. Policeman, neighbours, traffic wardens, passers-by, cars, buses; all were grist to Buster's mill.

Hyde Park was his realm. We'd throw sticks into the Serpentine and he'd leap prodigious distances in order to retrieve them. Crowds were drawn to the spectacle. Swimming back, Buster carried the sticks not sensibly balanced in the middle, but held at the end so they jutted forward and upright like a periscope. On his return to shore he would disperse the throng by power-showering them with spray. He shared his waters in other ways. He was a love machine. He loved the world and dispensed his joy freely. A sudden shower of

Buster's golden rain awakened many a sleeping sunbather. As for his other eliminations, he was ultra hygienic. With his immense paws he would back-heel his leavings, kicking them immense distances out of sight. His droppings dropped in all over Park Lane and Mayfair. Although born without a brain, Buster performed some astonishing feats of intelligence. Despite being happy at home, he ran away whenever the door was left open and sometimes when it wasn't. He could open it at will, or just burst through. He once disappeared for hours and was eventually found, at 10 p.m., on the third floor of the Army & Navy Club in Piccadilly. How he got through the revolving doors was a mystery to many high-ranking officers, German and otherwise.

Once, in an attempt to ease the burden of ownership, Buster was sent away for Police Dog training. He didn't graduate. The police dog handlers emerged from the ordeal with their hands raised and carrying white flags. Buster was given back.

Other careers were considered for him. A guide dog for the criminally insane, perhaps. But all to no avail. His love had to be endured to the end.

Henry Carr R.A. chanced by one day when I was painting. He asked if I planned to submit the picture for the R.A. Summer Exhibition. I didn't know you could enter. He explained anyone might enter up to three works. I duly submitted my picture. Weeks later, he asked if I'd been accepted.

'No,' I told him.

'Were you rejected, or did you get a D notice? he said.

I had no idea.

'Where is the picture?' he said.

It was just inside the studio door. He looked at the back of it. There was a large letter D in white chalk.

'You were accepted,' he said. 'That D means your picture was accepted but not hung because of lack of room.'

A jury of artists judge all works submitted to the Summer Exhibition. There are three verdicts: accepted; rejected; and the D notice, accepted but not hung. How about that! I'd been accepted. I was impressed. It might not impress you because the show has since become the annual whipping boy of the art world. The critics sneer. Yet the Royal Academy is the only major gallery in the world to encourage artists by opening its doors to them every year. The following year I had three paintings accepted.

Sydney Mews taught me two lessons. Count the bricks. And never underestimate the power of a pat on the back.

Chapter XXXII
The party of the second part.

The party at which I met Jack was not the only one I went to. There were others. There were also many hair-of-the-dog Sunday lunchtime meetings to be attended in a snug near Belgrave Square. There I would meet a friend or two, my equivalents of Dodger Green and Janaway. Other acquaintances would sometimes join us. One day I met a knight, Sir John Whitmore, a motor racing driver. He was arm-in-arm with his beautiful Swedish wife, Gunilla. He was not the first racing driver I came to know. Indeed, my Dodger Green - and later my best man and a godfather to my daughter - was Peter Jopp, a racing and rally driver. My Janaway - who, by coincidence, was known as the Janitor - although not a racing driver, was hugely important in motor sport at that time. He controlled the pit passes at Brands Hatch, a powerbase not exceeded until the reign of Bernie Ecclestone.

The sport was different back then. Somewhat.

The paddock at Brands consisted of wooden posts with corrugated tin sheets for a roof - a bit like Silverstone last time I went. If you arrived early, you could nab one of the slots where there were no holes in the roof. These were eagerly sought after. On my first visit I duly parked in a dry spot. Two spaces along, Stirling Moss was just parking. He bade me a courteous good morning. That made my day. Later I became friends with his secretary, Val, and came to know him. Indeed, he would sometimes join us in the snug on Sunday lunchtimes, though he never drank alcohol. I was in his pit at Goodwood on the day of the accident that sensationally ended his career and almost claimed his life. Oddly, it was the second accident he had that day.

It was Easter. Val and I drove to Scotland to visit her mother. We stayed one night and drove back, a six hundred-odd mile return journey, as you do. On Easter Monday we joined Stirling for breakfast at his hotel in Chichester. He was due to be featured on the cover of Time Magazine. An American writer from the title and his wife were at breakfast. They had been shadowing Stirling for a week, getting to know him for the magazine article. At the end of meal, as we prepared to leave for the circuit, the American's wife said she wouldn't come.

'I don't go to these things,' she said. 'I always bring bad luck.'

That day, Stirling's road car was a yellow Lotus Elite. As he reversed out of the hotel's private car park, the exhaust pipe caught the low wooden gatepost in the middle of the drive, and tore loose. I chanced to see it happen. I didn't see the major accident which, when it came, happened far from the pits. The reports came back that he was trapped in the car. One of Stirling's closest friends, David Haynes, who was also in the pit, said to me:

'Come on. I know where we're going.'

We left the circuit and drove to Chichester Hospital. It was completely deserted. No cars in the car park, no sign of anyone. In through the front door we went, no receptionist, no nurses, nobody on duty. Silent. We opened private office doors, looked everywhere. Maybe Stirling wouldn't be brought here? Maybe he'd been taken to another hospital? Then we came to one of those soft double doors that a gurney can be pushed through. We barged directly into an operating theatre. On the table, surrounded by a medical team was Stirling, naked except for his underpants.

'Get out, get out!' shouted the doctors.

We got out and went back outside to the still deserted car park. I was ashamed at our intrusion. I was also ashamed because of something else. Amid the drama, I'd noticed Stirling's underpants were tartan! And they were briefs, like swimming trunks. Tartan! How cool was that! I became acutely self-conscious of my own voluminous under-linen.

People began to arrive, the press, Stirling's parents, friends and other well-wishers. David and I returned to the circuit and, later, I drove Stirling's girl friend back to her parent's home in Epsom. We arrived just as the 9.0 p.m. TV news came on. It was full of the story, which made global headlines. I felt like I was in the eye of the storm, at the centre of the earth. It took Stirling - and me - a long time to recover.

Indeed later still, when I had married into the outskirts of the knight's world, the event would return to haunt me. Many famous racing drivers were regular visitors to John Whitmore's home, Orsett Hall in Essex. In those days, my wife and I spent almost as many weekends there as I had done at Jack and Moll's. One weekend, there was a virtual F1 starting grid in the house. I remember sitting in the study with Jim Clark, Graham Hill, Jackie Stewart, Bruce McLaren, Frank Gardener and a few others, taking tea. And all I could think of was, who is wearing tartan underpants? Well, apart from Jackie, obviously.

Two years before, another motor racing accident had taken a heavier toll. Among my closest friends at that time were Sonya, and her then husband, Keith. Her brother, Chris Bristow, drove for Stirling's team. Brother and sister were very close. On the Sunday of the race, Sonya, Keith and I were at Goodwood. We drove back to London and stopped at the Sun. It was the weekend of the Belgian Grand Prix at Spa. I phoned Reuters to get the result and asked about Chris. The chilling reply came:

'Are you a relative?'

Keith broke the news. In the disbelief of the moment, Sonya sat silent, dignified and calm. She was holding a piece of paper or card, perhaps the programme from Goodwood, which she wordlessly proceeded to tear into a thousand, tiny, minute shreds, her world disintegrating in her hands.

Ken Gregory, Stirling's manager, and manager of the team, would say much later:

'If he had survived, Chris Bristow almost certainly would have been a potential world champion. He was the early Schumacher of his day.'

Stirling, too, did not escape that weekend unscathed. He crashed heavily during practice breaking his nose and legs. That awful race was further marred by the death of another driver, Alan Stacey. Despite these, and many other tragedies, Jackie Stewart would later be ridiculed for daring to advocate an increase in motor racing safety.

Another motor racing legend I met in the snug was Les Leston. He too, was an advocate of motor racing safety, though not perhaps for quite the same noble reasons. Les was the 'godfather of the motor accessory business', which he had almost single-handedly created out of the post-war army surplus trade. He also became a godfather to my son, who surprisingly managed to get through the experience unscathed. When Les learned what I did for a living he asked me to do some work for him. His store in High Holborn was the Mecca for the go-faster stripe brigade. If you didn't have a Les Leston wood-rimmed steering wheel and driving gloves, well, you might as well be wearing a string vest - which I probably was. He asked me to prepare an ad campaign and enquired if I knew someone who could write the copy. I said I'd do it, never having written a word in my life.

But something else, unconnected with motor racing, had been going on.

Although I'd been handling artwork for major ad agencies for a few years, I'd never read any of the ads except to proof read them. They were of no interest. But I was also reading the New Yorker magazine. And recently I had begun to see ads that were not only eye catching, but original and witty. They were for an ugly little car called a VW Beetle - huh! - who would want one of those? Of course, I had no idea the ads were the work of an American advertising genius called Bill Bernbach who completely revolutionized the ad industry.

Bill Bernbach was the polar opposite of the English press lord, who had once famously declared that whenever a reader finished an article in one of his papers, they should end up hating someone. Today, of course, this art has been so perfected you can easily finish up hating the whole newspaper. Bill Bernbach wasn't like that. He not only wanted to sell the products he advertised. He wanted to win over the reader. He used charm, wit and intelligence to make you like a brand even if you didn't buy it. He knew the power of word-of-mouth recommendation. He thought good art and good writing made for good selling. Today, of course, all that has long since been derided as old-fashioned and middle-class. As the Times recently put it: '...advertising fell out of love with words'. But I was a Bernbach man through and through, even though I didn't know it.

The first ad I wrote for Leston - for anyone - contained in its headline, as you might expect, a wincing pun. Leston had a product, a holdall bag, covered in checkered tape and Leston logos, called a Track-sac. The whole page ad in Autosport magazine, showed a man wearing Leston racing overalls and carrying a Track-sac, climbing out of Leston's Ferrari road car. We photographed this at the motor racing circuit that was still in use at Crystal Palace. The headline read:

'He got the sack from Leston.'

I designed the ad by laying a piece of tracing paper over the latest VW ad in New Yorker. I even wrote the copy to the same word length. It looked terrific. So it should. I was copying the work of the great American art director, Helmut Krone, to whom I offer belated apologies. As for the pun in the headline, it no doubt made you wince, but it did have a sub-text, not immediately apparent. You see, Les had, at one time or another employed and then sacked practically everybody who worked in the motor accessory industry. He was a volatile employer.

Many a diligent worker exited 314 High Holborn going faster than when they went in.

The ads, Les said, made him famous. But the go-faster business did not always prosper. During one downturn Les left England and established a beachhead in Hong Kong. He lived there for some years, though what harm the colony had done him, I never knew. But while things were good they were, let us say, lively.

Every year Les organized the Grand Prix Drivers' XI cricket match against Lord Brabourne's XI - admission free, children half price! The match was held near Les's cottage in Kent. It was a Sunday event, held after the British Grand Prix, which in those days, was run on Saturday and hang the TV schedules. Real royalty as well as motor racing royalty attended the cricket. They all asked me the same question. How did I like working for Les? Actually, I liked it fine. True, he was explosive. But he could also be explosively funny. And he had become a close friend. Also, charmingly, Les told everyone he wrote his ads himself! That suited me. I didn't want to rise above my station, did I?

One weekend, Jim Clark was a guest at Leston's cottage. He had recently, and sensationally, won the Indianapolis 500, a feat Graham Hill, equally sensationally, would emulate the following year. During Clark's race, he had spun on the banking a full 360º and miraculously retained control, before going on to victory.

'How on earth did you do that? I asked.

'Rob Slotemaker,' he said.

Rob Slotemaker was a motor racing driver who ran a skid school at Zandvoort in Holland. He too later died in a racing crash. Part of Jimmy's Indianapolis prize was an American Ford Galaxy road car. We all packed into it to go out to dinner. In the foot well was a small, loose piece of unlikely floral patterned carpet.

'It's from home,' he replied to my question. 'I'm away such a lot, it reminds me of Scotland.'

He would be back home soon enough, for the last time, a grievous loss to those who knew him and to countless people who didn't.

Work went on.

'I'm on holiday next week, on a boat in the south of France,' said Les. 'I want you to come with me to plan the new catalogue.'

Fine, sounded great, Monte Carlo in springtime. The reality was twelve hours a day poring over tiny details and getting motion sickness from the yacht slapping against the harbour fenders while, through the portholes, what seemed like a Miss World pageant passed by outside.

We took time out now and then. We were lunching in a seafront café one day. In the harbour a U.S. aircraft carrier was anchored on a goodwill visit. Into the bar came a party of U.S.

sailors, eight or ten strong. The young waitress went to their table to take their order. They whistled and cat called her.

'We're from America, the greatest country in the world, and don't you forget it,' snarled one 18-year old.

'Haven't you got any decent American beer?' shouted another.

Outside the sun shone. The blue sea sparkled peaceably in the morning light. There were a handful of elderly local customers. They looked up.

'What are you looking at?' bellowed another ambassador.

'Effing frogs! If it wasn't for the good old U.S. of A., you'd all be speaking effing German,' yelled another.

I wondered what RSM Taylor would have done. I wondered what Les would do.

As a teenager he'd fought running street battles with Moseley's fascists in the east end of London. During the war he'd flown 30 RAF missions as a mid-upper turret gunner in Lancaster bombers. Turret gunners were notoriously vulnerable. Many was the time on return from a mission, so the gruesome story went, they had 'to hose the gunner out'. Les used to say that at the start of some missions, he was so hung over, they had to hose him in! Since then he'd built a business out of nothing. He'd become British F3, Saloon Car and GT Champion; won innumerable events including the Luxembourg GP; was works driver for F1 Connaught Team, F1 BRM Team,

Cooper, Aston Martin and Ford America; he'd held lap records at Brands Hatch, Silverstone, Goodwood, Crystal Palace, Rouen and Namur; and he'd competed in the Le Mans 24-hours five times; Monte Carlo Rally five times; RAC Rally four times; Tour de France twice; Alpine Rally four times; Leige/Sofia/Leige rally three times; Nurburgring 1000km three times.

If Les had had his mid-upper turret with him, the outcome of that lunch may have been different. Instead, we left the diplomats to their goodwill mission and walked out into the fresh air.

And the lesson from the Leston years?

Well, I learned to spell incorrigible. And one other thing happened while I was working with Les. I received a phone call from Bill Bernbach.

Chapter XXXIII
Quiet days in cliché.

The phone call I received was not from Bill Bernbach personally, but from his representative on earth, John Withers, creative director of Doyle, Dane, Bernbach. The New York agency had opened a London office in Baker Street. They ran a whole page ad in the advertising trade press, looking for copywriters. I replied, saying I didn't want a job, but if they needed any freelance work done until they found a writer, I'd be pleased to help. I was in Les's office in Holborn when John Withers called and asked me to go and see him. The following day, armed with my portfolio of three Leston ads, I went along. Have you ever been numb with nerves? It's not unpleasant. It's nothing like being nervous. It's more like being dead. John Withers looked at the work and said okay. I believe his actual words were:

'You seem to have an individual style.'

Translated, this probably meant he was under extreme deadline pressure and any port in storm would do. He briefed

257

me on a Polaroid campaign, saying he needed concepts the following day. He then added:

'How much do you charge?'

Charge? Did people get paid for this? Up to that time I'd never charged Leston anything. Les, for his part, had never offered. A pause ensued. John Withers then said:

'If it's too much, I'll fly a writer in from New York.'

'May I phone you back?'

'Sure.'

There was a travel agency on the corner of Baker and Blandford Streets. I went in and asked the cost of a return air ticket to New York. I phoned the price through to John Withers.

'Fine,' he said.

That figure became the yardstick for all future transactions. Such comfort as I sit in today is due entirely to the absence, in those innocent days, of budget airlines. Thank you, B.A., or B.O.A.C as it was.

There was then the small matter of doing the work. I stayed up half the night, whisky bottle to hand. I'm sure if I'd owned a green eyeshade and shirtsleeve armbands I would have worn them like they do in the movies. The following day, number than numb, deader than dead, I delivered the work.

'Fine,' said the ever-courteous John Withers. 'Now I have another job for you.'

I continued to freelance for DDB, its offshoots and other ad agencies and direct clients for the next several decades. But it was the second DDB job that was a turning point.

'The job,' John said, 'is for Quaker Oats. And here at DDB we work in teams. Come in tomorrow and I'll introduce you to your art director.'

I didn't like to say my normal way of working with art directors was to trace over their previous ads and leave it at that. But the idea of help was immensely appealing. The following morning, with a real sense of relief I said hello to Pete Kettle. In a rush of humility and with the distinct feeling I was masquerading as an impostor, I told him I'd only ever written three ads and was here under false pretences, in view of which, I would rely utterly upon him to do the majority of the work, whatever it was. Pete, ever one to lift one's spirits, said:

'I've only been here two weeks myself.'

Pete didn't know it, but he was about to be burdened with a long friendship he hadn't expected when he got off the train from Lewes that morning. Was it The Big Sleep, that Bogart movie, where someone gets inexplicably shot and when asked who the murderer was the author, Raymond Chandler, said he had no idea? Pete and I, in our first outing together, went one better than that. The job was to write a competition for the back of a Quaker Oats cereal pack. Our conversation was succinct.

'Ever written a competition?'

'No.'

'Have you?'

'No.'

'Ever won one?'

'No,'

'You?'

'No.'

'Ever entered one?'

'No,'

'You?'

'No.'

'Ever read one?'

'No,'

'You?'

'No.'

As I recall, we produced a competition so complex neither of us knew its solution. The client loved it. No one dared question it for fear of making a fool of themselves. A whole generation of school children was condemned to stumble through life, glowing with porridgy health, but forever bemused by its promotion.

Art director, illustrator, painter, novelist, that's Pete Kettle. If he could do maths he'd be a polymath. He has strings of awards: New York International Clio; D&AD Silver; Tokyo Art Director's Club Silver; many D&AD yellow pencils; the list goes on. He partnered some of the greatest copywriters of the day: David Abbott, Tony Brignull, Malcolm Gluck, John Salmon. Why he worked with me was one of adland's minor mysteries. The mystery deepened when he resigned from lucrative and steady employment and went freelance. The reason he did so was to give more time to his painting and illustration work. To supplement that income, he teamed up with me as my art director, more or less permanently.

Another tragic error of judgement.

At that period we were, I believe, one of only two full-time creative consultancies in London. The word consultant, I should point out, had not yet achieved the risible connotations it has today. In fact, I thought it sounded quite posh. After all, we had the Leston account. The future looked rosy. As for the other consultancy they, with the aid of one of their brothers, rapidly transformed themselves into one of the world's most successful advertising agencies. And the copywriting part of the team went on to become one of the world's leading collectors of modern art. Pete Kettle suggested this stellar achievement might have something to do with talent. But I blamed Mum. It wasn't my fault I hadn't got a brother.

My secret ambition was to get advertising work into the annual D&AD show and have paintings hung in the Royal Academy Summer Exhibition in the same year. It never happened. Well, at least, not yet. Meanwhile our ad work was attracting a certain amount of attention. We were approached on several, indeed many occasions, to join agencies. Always I declined, including turning down one offer of such generosity I - along with other members of my family - later came to doubt my sanity. I decline to name the other party, not out of discretion after all this time, but because I don't enjoy the sensation of my eyes brimming with the tears of folly.

The glue that held Pete and I together was painting.

I admire and respect his paintings. His work is original, intelligent and exquisitely crafted. You can tell a Pete Kettle picture at a glance across a room. It is no wonder to me that his work is bought by discerning and knowledgeable collectors. It is a wonder to me that he is not more celebrated. Yet even that is not strictly true. I do know the reason. One year he had a one-man show in Covent Garden. The day after the private view a venerable art critic arrived unannounced. It is to his credit that he showed interest in an 'unknown' artist. He admired the work and said to Pete:

'You have no absolutely no chance whatsoever of breaking into the current art establishment. Its doors are forever closed to you and others like you.'

Many painters know that to be true. I suppose it was ever thus. As the Spanish say, the road to heaven is heaven. The consoling factor is the work is more important than the market.

Pete's art might be called imaginative realism. He can both draw and paint, redundant skills in some eyes. Above all, there is imagination at work, thought made manifest, ideas revealed that could only be expressed through paint. I believe his work lacks only one thing. Advocacy. With the right critic on his side it wouldn't take long before you would be telling me about him, not the other way round. As the owner of several of his pictures, of course, I'm biased, but I have nothing against bias as long as it is accurate and fair.

Between the viewer and any painting lies a prism of received opinion that is as much a part of the artwork as the paint. The best critics guide us through this refraction and help us to see for ourselves. But just as light travels in waves and particles, so critical opinion moves in mysterious ways. And in art, it seems to me, the interference pattern that forms on the far side of the light experiment's famous two slits looks suspiciously like a barcode.

I wish I had consulted Uncle Jack about this. I would have valued his opinion.

Of course, I've also had huge help from Pete with my own painting that, compared to his, is simply representational. I'm wary of the risk involved in representation, the potential pitfall of achieving nothing but the 'tame delineation of a given spot'. Yet I'm equally wary when I hear talk of 'the inner world', a place so often spoken about you'd think you could buy a ticket - b-boomp! b-boomp! - and go there.

I think Oscar Wilde had a point when he said:

'The true mystery of the world is the visible, not the invisible.'

Perhaps art should be subjected to scientific enquiry, to determine what 'art' is. This is not an original idea, of course. How could it be done? I don't know. What is the scientific method? To count what can be counted and make countable that which can't be counted?

Come to think of it, you could start by counting the bits of bush.

There is one thing, though, I love unreservedly about much modern art. That is the prose used to describe it. This has rightly been honoured in many publications:

'Inevitably in the endeavour to unite intention with means, pathos appropriates nature; a bid for possession humanises a process of integral monstrosity which is in diametrical opposition to man's disposition to idealising its forms.'

Sublime. It calls to mind Bertie Wooster's thoughts on a similar passage put to him by his fiancée of the moment, Florence Craye:

'All perfectly true, no doubt; but not the sort of thing to spring on a lad with a morning head.'

Painting was one of the 'ties that bind' but it wasn't the only one. Pete had read everything, seen everything and listened to everything. Poetry, books, film, theatre, opera, music, he was -

is - encyclopedic in his knowledge. He knew all the things I wanted to know. He was also useful for revision purposes. He drinks moderately and, unlike his copywriting partner, his knowledge does not regularly ebb away on an evening tide of claret.

Yes, his company was one of the better things about being in advertising. That, and being indoors out of the rain.

Chapter XXXIV
Moving times.

We had moved the business from the basement in Bruton Street to rooms in No 1, York Street, W1, a town house of a certain, shabby, faded elegance. Our landlord was The Thomas Wall Trust, of Wall's Sausages fame. This became our permanent London base from then on.

On the home front, your correspondent lived at The Rising Sun as long as they would let him. The arrangement suited him well. It was rent-free and it had built in laundry facilities, courtesy of 'I'm here'. Also, as it happened, living at home imposed no constraints upon the young gentleman's lifestyle - although it wasn't called a lifestyle yet, it was just your life, mate.

You see, he had a bolt hole. Another regular in the Belgravia snug, a close friend of Stirling Moss, was Herb Jones, an American architect who lived and worked in England. His work took him to Yorkshire during the week, leaving his flat in Sloane Avenue, Chelsea, unlived in except at weekends. This seemed a shame, so an arrangement was made to the satisfaction of both parties. I used it in the week.

Do you believe in coincidences? Neither did I. But they can happen. One evening, after a pleasant dinner with a new acquaintance, a young lady from North Surrey I believe, she and I went back to 'my' flat. After suitable preliminaries, she took her repose upon the divan and when the ceiling swam into her field of vision, she said:

'Does Herb Jones still live here?'

Not exactly the sort of wake-up call you need at bedtime. I had no idea Herb roamed the Surrey hills. It was pure coincidence. Fortunately, it was the only thing pure about her, if memory serves. To this day, when in SW3, I avoid passing Nell Gwynne House. Too many ghosts. There were other shadows too, gradually appearing.

Mum had been stricken with a cruel affliction, tic douloureux. This is a sudden, severe, stabbing pain lasting a few seconds, on one side of the face. It is caused by pressure on the trigeminal nerve. I'd only heard of the complaint in one of Charles Dickens's novels. Was it Sam Weller who was a sufferer? Mum had complained for some time, but I had no idea how bad the condition was until one day I was with her in the kitchen in the Sun. She was cooking and was suddenly thrown sideways as if she had been punched in the face. It was shocking to see, let alone experience. Treatment at that time seemed to consist only of injections of vitamin B12. These went on for years. Mum eventually had to have an operation with the risk that her face would 'drop' on that side. Fortunately it didn't.

But the years were catching up. You can't run a pub forever. Once again, my sister Margaret and her husband John stepped into the breach. In a spectacular display of understated generosity, they organized and funded a flat for Mum and Reg to move into, rent-free for life. How they did this, I'll never know. I'm not sure they know.

The leaving party that was thrown before Mum and Reg left The Rising Sun was amazing. You had to be there to believe it. Every important person in the world was there. It was nothing but A-list celebrities: Uncle Jack, Auntie Win, Ethel and Joan, Marg and John, Rose, big Pat Brady. Never, even on the wildest football Saturday had more people crammed into the four bars. They drank their 'gin and its', wept into their beers, refilled them and wept again. They sang the songs of the day long into the night, the unashamed pub folk songs of the time and drank and happily wept again. There was a special license extension until midnight and when it finally came, Mum and Reg called time for the last time. The bell was rung, hands were wrung. On the pavements outside, tears and hugs and handshakes slowed the nighttime traffic like the smogs of years gone by.

'Hurry up please it's time.'

But this time there was no hurry.

'...Goonight...Goonight...Ta ta...Goonight...'

I've never been in the Sun since. It has changed its name - and its ways - many times since then, changes Mum and Reg could not have imagined. For her part, Mum never went back. Thirty-four years was enough. The past is flexible. As it fades, we revise it to suit ourselves.

In another move, I bought a home of my own.

The south-facing view from the one-bed roomed, ninth floor flat in the block called Lords' View, by Lord's cricket ground, took my breath away. It overlooked, in the foreground, an immense and magnificent power station that would soon be decommissioned. The square sectioned chimneystack of the building towered over everything. The chimney was so big a double-decker bus could have been driven round the top rim. 'The monstrosity', other residents called it but I loved it. The whole power station was a splendid brick structure and I watched as, in a gross act of civic vandalism, it was demolished brick by brick. It should have been saved like Tate Modern. But who was there to listen back then? I painted the building repeatedly before it vanished. Beyond the power station lay the goods and marshalling yards of Marylebone Station. There were trains everywhere! Beyond the trains, the low-lying valley of the Thames could be discerned before the land rose again in the far Surrey hills. High above the valley, from east to west, far enough away not to be heard, aircraft came - one a minute - on their final approach into Heathrow. The view suited my outlook. I loved it.

The flat, so I planned, was to be my launch pad into the swinging era that I'd heard so much about, but felt so left out of. No more sharing ceilings with anybody, thank you very much. On the evening of the day I signed the purchase completion forms, I met my wife. She had come to England from Sweden for a holiday and to visit her half-sister, Gunilla, the knight's wife.

The first day we stepped out together was memorable, not only to me, but to most of west London. I was, of course, immensely proud to be seen with the young lady in question. There was, however, a slight drawback for one of my reticent disposition. My companion was wearing wooden clogs. This footwear may have been high fashion in Stockholm's Kungsgatan, but clogs hadn't been worn in these parts since the Great Fire of London. The din was incredible. It was like walking along with a horse. Our progress was also notable because the only real horse in this part of London belonged to Steptoe and Son, well-known TV rag-and-bone men of the day. Many eyes were turned towards us expecting to see Albert and Harold. Instead of a horse and cart, they saw a vision that as far as I was concerned had stepped right out of dream. And when, later that week at a romantic candlelit dinner, my companion inadvertently burped and blew the candle out, well, the night became dark but the future became clear. The one-bed roomed flat must become home for two.

It was some while after this that Boswell's famous Dr. Johnson came to mind. The renowned Doctor, you will recall, once observed that: 'No man but a blockhead ever wrote except for money.' Well, Doctor, allow me to introduce myself. I'm the blockhead you presumably had in mind. What I mean is, at some stage I started to keep a diary. This practice - unpaid - should be curbed, certainly for ordinary people. Only citizens of distinction should be permitted to keep journals. Why? Because one day some fool might publish all these diaries of the nobodies. And to unleash that much tedium on an already polluted planet would be environmentally hazardous. Diaries are dangerous. They lead lives of their own. They take you over. A diary writes you. 'Keep a diary, and one day it will keep you', is a myth. There is only one reason to keep a diary and that is my reason.

Revenge.

Revenge pure and simple. You see, ever since I started, you are all in it. Every day, everyone I meet auditions for a part. The odder you are, the more I like it. I'm not talking about a sanitized maunder, full of discretion, such as you're reading at the moment. I'm talking gloves off, down and dirty, every

271

available bodice ripped, the real me, exposed for what I truly am, the character assassinator who masks his venom beneath a cloak of decorum. Wouldn't you like to know what I really thought about you? Of course you would. But you never shall. So far, I've written literally millions of words - regrettably not millions of literary words - but what the wretched oeuvre lacks in quality, it makes up in quantity. And not one word shall you ever see. Why? Because, in a masterstroke of vengeance, I've donated the lot to one of the world's great university libraries.

Take that, Mr. Guy Boas! Take that, all you teachers, examiners and jurors who condemned me to the cul-de-sac of Transitus. And when, in time to come, Transitus, Sloane School, the very stones themselves are gone, I'll be safely tucked away beneath another seat of learning, resident under dreaming spires, at the apogee of knowledge itself. And you lot shall be forgotten! Take that, I say again! My diaries, along with those of a thousand other blockheads who have vainly scratched out their livings, will lie undisturbed, hidden from the prying eyes of the world for one reason and one reason alone. They are of no interest to anyone.

As someone put it:

'Such observations are not useful for anything...they have no shape...are based on no hypothesis...contain no insights... make no connections...Observation is of value only when the observer is obsessed by a problem, and when that obsession is

272

sustained…by (say) fear, vanity, competition, money, curiosity, desperation or a deadline.'

I could hear the courteous boredom in the university librarian's voice when I offered my bequest.

'Do you accept such things? I said.

'Yes, of course,' he said.

In the momentary silence that followed, I fancied I could hear the word 'blockhead' hanging in the air. He'd heard it all before. My gold was turning to dross even before I'd handed it over. The great institutions are no doubt swamped with scribblers wanting to donate their life's work in a vain stab at immortality.

But I wasn't put off. Who knows, I reasoned, one day the world may want to know the price of cotton wool balls in Boots the Chemist, High Wycombe, on 8 June 1979. Or why the milkman didn't arrive on the day the dog was sick into my Wellington boot. When that happens, world, I shall come into my own. It's all there. The dross is in the detail. And despite the inordinate length and the waste of paper and good ink - Mont Blanc Royal Blue, since you ask - my regret is not the writing of it, but that I didn't start it earlier. I missed out on some good stuff.

My wife, like her half-sister and other Swedish ex-pats we knew, spoke good English. But there was, inevitably, a year or so of transition to full command of the language. One star, on being asked where the dishcloth was, replied:

'It's over neath the wash basement.'

On another occasion she saw a road sign which read: To the coast.

'Britain's an island, isn't it?' she said.

'Yes.'

'So the sign could point anywhere?'

'Well, yes, but...'

I missed recording many such gems because I hadn't at that time settled into to my unreliable history. What's that word - log something, logorrhea is it - that means excessive or incoherent talking? Well, I had caught the writing form of it. Don't confuse this with blogorrhea, the online form of the disease. The written form of the complaint only truly manifests itself in handwriting. The hand written word is a drawing, a self-portrait in line. The spelling mistakes, the crossings out, the false starts, the scratchings, the errors, the blots, the inky-fingered-ness, all reveal the writer in a way no typescript can.

So it was I missed a small part of history, but not nearly as much as was ignored in the case of Uncle Reg. The tic douloureux eventually left Mum, but dementia lay in wait for Reg. It started during his retirement years. First came the forgetfulness; then the wandering off; the disappearing; the being brought home by the police or by ambulance. Then a mercifully brief hospitalization in a gibbering, howling, 'snake pit' of sadness, staffed by saints. (To this day, I wonder what the resident psychologist made of 'Kraigs-ghy-fagin-agin-laager'.)

Finally, came the inevitable last days spent in a care home.

Margaret, John and I sat with him at the end. We listened as his breathing became ever more stertorous and laboured. I held his hand as he had held mine as a child.

'It could be any time,' said the nurse.

We left to go back to tell Mum, who lived nearby. By the time we got there, they'd phoned to say he had died ten minutes after we left.

Reginald Osborne, footballer, publican, husband, soldier, stepfather, had served in the First World War. Never once had I asked him about it. Where he served, what action, if any, he saw. It's all blank. He never spoke of it. His stepson, the history man, never asked. All I know is he didn't die in it.

Couples often die in pairs, but not this time. The soldier had gone, but Mum soldiered on in tranquility for a while. She had home help, of course, and her helper came to be a remarkable help to all of us. As Mum's ability to cope alone declined, Margaret and I often suggested she should move into a care home. She wouldn't hear of it. Then one day, Mum suddenly announced she would move. It seemed her home help also worked at a nearby Catholic care home. She had convinced Mum she'd like it there. Margaret took Mum to see the home.

Mum liked what she saw and moved in. The long slow sadness of decline, serves a purpose. As the loved one becomes less lovely, love cools into habit, protecting those left behind from the worst of grief as loss turns into release.

Chapter XXXV
Four entries and an exit.

<u>Friday 21 January</u>

"Mother is in ward F3 of the West Middlesex Hospital. The room is big, busy and bustling. It's a nice room, wide spaced. There are many people; flowers everywhere, even on the bright blue curtain dividers. I worry in case I won't recognize her. Age strips identity along with everything else. Many of the patients are very elderly. One is retching into a bowl. It isn't Mum. Other faces are white and flaccid. Then I see her in the corner of the room, sitting up in a chair with an attached table. On its surface are two empty glasses. Her false teeth are out and the excessive caved-in look this imparts, adds to her age. She is talking or mumbling to herself, moving her jaws as if speaking but I'm not sure if it isn't just a driven reflex. She knows me but doesn't know me, speaking as if I'd always been in the room. She has, in her decline, passed back beyond the age of self-consciousness, into an earlier sentience and in making this regression has lost her depression. She is alert, but in a reduced manner and her talk is of earlier events in her life. 'Have you done the windows?' she asks. To anyone who hadn't shared her life this would be incomprehensible, but I knew what she meant. In the pub, it was one of the tasks at closing time to go round all the bars locking doors, sweeping up and especially closing and locking all the windows. These were fanlight affairs high above the main panes of glass. A burglar, who must have been agile, once breached our defences in this way and it was mandatory to close our ranks against him and his kind every night. The opened windows leaned into the bar rooms at an angle of about 30^0 and they opened and closed with a screw mechanism. This screw was reached by a long key the length of a walking stick. You engaged the tee-piece at the top and then turned the handle at the other end and this wound the window closed. In order that the shaft of the key could turn, it ran through a red wooden handle shaped to fit the hand. This tool was kept in the tiny office, just inside the door on the right. I can hear the squeak and click of it in action. I can feel it in my hands reliable, stoutly made, a walking stick of my youth and of my Mother's middle life. 'Yes,' I say to her. 'I've done the windows.' She nods in satisfaction. When I leave she sits, her jaws moving ceaselessly, soundlessly."

Friday 18 February

"Mrs. Purdy's gone. And Mrs. Collingwood. Both gone. One after the other. One, one day, one the next. Sad isn't it.' This

278

is Pam speaking, one of the saintly helpers in Nazareth House, the care home. I can't recall the two departed souls, though I suspect Mrs. Purdy was the one with the two sticks who would, every now and then regain full use of her legs, stand upright and belay about her using her sticks as cudgels. This engendered a swiftness of movement in her fellow inmates they hadn't enjoyed for half a century. Mrs. Two Sticks as she was known, would sit by the door of the TV room, a hellhole of full-volume noise. In the days when Mum was still mobile I would escort her past the good lady. Mrs. Two Sticks would then heave her great bulk towards us, saying, 'I'm coming too.' She spoke in an accent so thick I never knew where she was from. It was months before I could decipher the words. I'd smile courteously in reply and, Mother, clutching my arm would skedaddle past. 'Watch out for those sticks,' she'd say. Well, the sticks have been laid to rest, if indeed it was her, but Mum soldiers on. She's heading for 87 and tonight was bright and newly coiffed. There are two ladies in the infirmary with her and when I knocked and put my head around the door I thought they were all dead. One, a dark skinned body lay with her head hanging over the side of the mattress gazing upward with silent eyes. In the red corner a whiter geriatric was supine, whiter than the sheets on which she lay, surely she must be gone. Mum was in the middle bed, propped up by a bank of blue pillows, her head hung down on her breastbone, her hair done, her face undone. 'Hello Mum', I bellow and up comes the topknot, vertebra clicking like castanets. She's instantly fully awake. 'Hello, dear, you've come then, it seems ages since I saw you and they've been saying all day, Jimmy's coming, but I thought to myself how come they know and, oh dear, they seem to know more about it than I do and you are looking well and I haven't seen Margaret but she's busy, what with downstairs...' I pop a boiled sweet in her mouth and she continues her monologue sounding like Bill and Ben, the Flower Pot men. I sneak a glance over my shoulder. The two dead have withdrawn under their sheets like tortoises. The nurse, Sister Winifred, arrives, two large angelic wings attached to her shoulders, and gives me tea and biscuits. 'I've had gastric flu,' says Mum, making me wish I hadn't dunked my biscuit in my tea."

Tuesday 8 March

"Margaret had a call from Sister Winifred saying Mum was not expected to last the night. She immediately went to the home and found Mum in the semi-conscious sleepy state that was to be expected. I had felt, when I saw her last Friday, that she was far-gone. I'm not outwardly upset, nor inwardly for that matter. It's due time and I squarely consider it a release. What I feel more consciously than sorrow is a kind of seriousness of mood, a stilling of humour, a pause in front of something profound and unknown. There is, as yet, no sense of loss. Habit hasn't yet been altered or interrupted. Bound as I am by the iron hoops of routine I probably shan't feel sad until Friday, when I'm next due to visit. I've been to see her every Friday for 12 years or more. I've said before, I want her at peace. It looks now as if I'm to have my wish."

<u>Wednesday 9 March</u>

"Mum lived through the night but not the day. I arrived at Nazareth House at 5.15pm to find Sister Winifred sitting by her, the curtains drawn around the bed. Mother was far gone, breathing laboriously, mouth agape and the sound of death's rattle in her throat. That objectionable noise! It makes you want to cough to clear your own throat. I joined the watch with Sister. Mother lay with her arms inside the covers and her knees drawn up. I could not take her hand so I rested my hand on the covers on her knee. Sister said: 'She's been waiting for you to come.' I wiped spittle from Mother's lips in a timorous show of nursing. Marie, one of the young staff, came in and showed me up. She took holy water and cleansed the mouth, wetting the tongue, which was like parchment, cleaning the lips, holding Mum with no disgust, just concern and care. Time passed. I sat with a cup of tea, not liking to look at the labouring face, trying to be detached. An hour or more went by then came a change in the breathing. Her mouth closed and she breathed through the nose, trying to exhale through the mouth, puffing, her cheeks filling with air. Her left eye was quite closed but her right eye was half open though unseeing. After a few moments of the new breathing pattern she reverted to the old, the rattle returning to replace the wheezing. Now it was near 7.0 pm and Sister returned. Throughout my stay the staff were looking in, worried, concerned. The throat noise became deeper, filling the room. The effort of breathing was growing more arduous. We cling to life. Now Marie and two other young girl helpers were with us, tearful and murmuring. Sister Winifred knelt by the head of the bed, a pile of tissues to hand, wiping, cleaning. She put the reading light on and to our surprise the light caused a flicker of eye movement. The eyes opened for a moment and Mum turned her head slightly towards my side of the bed. 'She can see you, she sees you,' said Sister and perhaps she did. The other girls were all kneeling now, all crying. 'I can see the silver tear,' said one. This, legend has it, being the last tear which leaves its mark forever on the cheek. Now the breathing became less, each exhalation more a sigh and Sister began the litany, repeated time after time: 'Jesus, Mary Mother of God… Jesus, Mary, Mother of God… incanting to the slightly moving face, while both our hands stroked her hair. Her eyes opened wide one last time, unseeing, and she became still, relaxing into peace, a small nerve jumping near her chin. She died at 7.40pm."

Chapter XXXVI
The end of the beginning.

So there are our dates, the ones we wondered about at the beginning, 1896-1983, brief enough indeed. We cremated mother at a service in west London and afterwards took the ashes in an urn out to the gardens and with some 'dismal ceremonies and incantations' threw her away under a tree. The death of your second parent puts you head of the queue and the event left me stilled yet, of course, still writing. But that's enough for the moment.

The time has come for another parting.

Of course, I could ramble on endlessly, but you've suffered enough. Just before we say goodbye, though, and you stagger off for some counselling, let me sum up what you've just put yourself through.

My aim has been to fill in some of the events that happened during the years before my own nuclear family detonated about my ears. To tell, in other words, of those irrecoverable days, in that brief springtime when I was temporarily a person before becoming, first a husband, and then a parent. Such as it is, what you've read is the answer to the unasked question from my own children:

'What did you do before you met Mum?'

Well, now they - and you - know. Sort of.

I suppose, in a way, I've written this for them. And it has just occurred to me that what I'm now writing is a dedication. Dedications, of course, are supposed to be at the front of books. Typical! Here we are in the guard's van, up at the back, and I've only just thought of it. Still, better late than never. So, now, to them and - while I'm at it - to the whole family, let me formally declare that I dedicate this book to the lot of youse.

Actually, something else comes to mind.

If they had asked that first question, they would almost certainly have also asked how I came to meet their mother, the most important person in my life.

Well, the story of 'When and where and how/we met, we wooed, and made exchange of vow...' is simply told.

Armed, as I was saying, with my new flat I set about putting it to good use. What girl in her right mind could resist a breath-taking view overlooking an industrial power station, to say nothing of a railway goods yard thrown in for good measure? On the evening of the day I signed the lease, I called a girl I knew to ask her out to dinner. She already had a date, but she said Gunilla's half-sister was staying with her.

'Why not take her out?'

The apartment where she was staying was in a block high above Notting Hill. It was sufficiently luxurious to intimidate the timid. The hushed lift was poetry in motion. It worked on many levels. The architect had spared no expense. The building was full of son et lumière, pure theatre. As I emerged from the elevator, through the window on the landing, a starlit night outshone the lights of London far below. Silently I moved across the deep pile carpeting to the door and pressed the bell.

There was a pause before I became aware of the music.

Softly, the unforgettable opening crescendo of Richard Strauss's, Thus Spake Zarathrustra filled the air, each chord timed to the half-heard approaching footsteps. The door opened and a burst of radiant light blazed out, piercing the very heart of darkness. The music climaxed and segued into the opening riff of John Coltrane's, A Love Supreme. And there before me stood a 'designated area of outstanding natural beauty', the 20-year old, 'drenchingly beautiful' Marianne von Feilitzen.

And we lived happily ever after.

Well, one out of two ain't bad.

Printed in the United Kingdom
by Lightning Source UK Ltd.
108775UKS00002B/26